Working for a Better World

WORKING
FOR A
BETTER
WORLD

Dr. Carolyn Y. Woo
CEO and President, Catholic Relief Services

Our Sunday Visitor Publishing Division
Our Sunday Visitor, Inc.
Huntington, Indiana 46750

Copyright © 2015 by Catholic Relief Services. Published 2015.

20 19 18 17 16 15   1 2 3 4 5 6 7 8 9

ISBN 978-1-61278-814-2 (Inventory No. T1620)
eISBN: 978-1-61278-374-1
LCCN: 2015931310

Cover design: John Lucas
Cover image: Shutterstock

PRINTED IN THE UNITED STATES OF AMERICA

CONTENTS

By Fr. Theodore M. Hesburgh, C.S.C.

Meet my friend. Dr. Carolyn Woo makes that easy as she visits us in the pages of her new book, *Working for a Better World*. It is difficult to be totally objective about one's friends, and I don't claim to be. I do want you to get to know Carolyn Woo, though, because she is courageous, competent, and committed. She is clearly led by the Holy Spirit: mind and heart. Meet a daughter, sibling, wife, and mother: a person who lives what she teaches and in the process has come to see all as neighbor.

When communism took over mainland China, Carolyn Woo's parents left their ancestral homes for Hong Kong. Thus, she identifies with refugees because her family was displaced and had to start over. The efforts of Carolyn's family and nanny were complemented by her education with the Maryknoll Sisters, whose witness and prayers strengthened her for a life of believing in God, in her neighbor, and in herself.

When she began her freshman year at Purdue University, she had enough resources for only one year of study. A secure future was a dream and a goal. Here again the Church in the form of St. Thomas Aquinas Center at Purdue supplied a life-giving community for her. Purdue University was a godsend for Carolyn Woo, not the least because it brought David Bartkus, her eventual husband and partner in faith, into her life. Beyond the scholarships, education, leadership opportunities, mentoring, and friendships, Purdue became a physical, emotional, and spiritual home for her, David, and eventually their two children, Ryan and Justin.

After nearly twenty-five years at Purdue, Carolyn and her family pulled up stakes for Notre Dame, a move about mission, not ambition. She and David felt that the Holy Spirit was asking her to accept this invitation. Carolyn Woo served as Dean of Notre Dame's Mendoza College of Business for nearly fifteen years.

In her years as dean, Carolyn's faith, vision of what a truly Catholic education entails, understanding of management, and mission-driven leadership moved the college steadily forward. During her last two years, Notre Dame's undergraduate business education was ranked number one in the nation. Our Mendoza College of Business has continued to hold this designation each year since Carolyn Woo left for Catholic Relief Services. This continued success of the College is attributable to the structures she put in place and the gifted people she gathered and inspired.

Carolyn and her faculty repeatedly stressed to students that they were being educated to advance the common good or, better, to build God's kingdom. So she recognized the Holy Spirit's involvement in 2003 when CRS asked her to join its board, and when it appealed to her to leave Notre Dame effective January 2012. It was time for Carolyn to follow what she had been urging students to do — i.e., to use one's blessings to better the lives of one's neighbors. So in her late fifties Carolyn Woo surrendered to being uprooted again by the Holy Spirit, this time to lead the official international humanitarian organization of the Catholic community in the United States.

The God who beckoned awaited her in Baltimore. As Carolyn has come to realize, God has been there each step of the way. Though international development is not her expertise, CRS has five thousand amazing employees with extensive knowledge on which she relies. Just as she did here at Notre Dame, Carolyn Woo serves her new community with humility and a commitment to excellence. Even now, CRS is being strengthened by Carolyn Woo's faith, her vision of what it is to be the bearer of the good news of the Gospel, her management expertise, and the examples of her diligence and persistence.

My friend is not just giving, though. She is constantly humbled by what she sees, by what she is learning with CRS, and she is deeply grateful for that. CRS's gifted, selfless, and zealous colleagues teach her much about discipleship. She is awed. Joy and goodness abound in many places where needs are the greatest. The colossal and complex needs of our brothers and sisters around the world are teaching her to pray with even greater fervor: "Come, Holy Spirit"; and "Today is a workday, Father, Son, Holy Spirit, and Blessed Mother. We all have to show up." My friend's faith tells her that suffering does not make sense unless we believe that God is both part of it and on the other side of it. There is a manifest need in all of us for hope, sustenance, and human contact. As we share such gifts with our neighbors, we are at the intersections where miracles happen and angels are encountered.

In 1934, when I entered Notre Dame as a freshman, barely seventeen years old, I began praying, "Come, Holy Spirit," and turning for help to Mary, Mother of us all, and Mother of Our Savior. I could stand near the statue of the poor shepherd girl, Bernadette, at our Grotto or gaze at Mary on the Dome. The Holy Spirit and Mary have never failed me.

Carolyn Woo began her college career young and feeling very much alone. With no one else to depend on, she regularly invited the Holy Spirit into her day. From her

Notre Dame office in the Mendoza College of Business she could plainly see Mary atop the Golden Dome. Carolyn often turned to her there and at the Grotto for clarity and courage. Carolyn likes to say that mediocrity was no way to serve our Blessed Mother.

I can't say enough about this good lady, Carolyn Woo; but, as I look out my window toward the Blessed Mother at the Golden Dome, I do pray that you meet my friend and the neighbors that we have around the world in the pages of her new book, *Working for a Better World.*

FR. THEODORE M. HESBURGH, C.S.C., *was a priest of the Congregation of Holy Cross and served as the president of the University of Notre Dame from 1952 to 1987. He passed away on February 26, 2015, at the age of 97, as this book was being prepared to go to press. Dr. Woo was able to visit Fr. Ted five days before his passing, and he offered her a blessing and reiterated the importance of serving the poor. The Gospel reading for his funeral Mass was from Matthew 25.*

Part I

God Has Always Been There

CHAPTER ONE

"... I Would Get Down on My Knees and Pray"

It was in Cambodia that I saw it, a crucifix like so many around the world, but with one major difference — Christ was missing one leg. For sale at the Jesuit Refugee Services Peace Café, it was made by victims of land mines, many of whom are missing a limb. It was touching to see how they claimed Christ, His suffering and His triumph, for their own.

Earlier that day I had visited the Tuol Sleng Genocide Museum, one of the mass graves monuments to the horrific killings that occurred here in the 1970s. There I had looked at a majestic tree, whose shade was welcoming in the intense heat. A sign on it read, "Killing tree against which executioners beat children."

It was overwhelming.

How had God prepared the path that brought me here, that made me confront such evil, such injustice?

I thought back to an uncommonly low-key afternoon in the dean's office of the Mendoza College of Business at the University of Notre Dame two years earlier. It was the Tuesday before Thanksgiving, and I was looking forward to having our two sons home for the holidays.

I returned a phone call to Bishop George Thomas of Helena, Montana, who was chairing the search committee for the CEO-President of Catholic Relief Services (CRS). I had just finished my second three-year term as a board member, and I was honored to have been invited to be part of this committee dedicated to finding the right person to head the official international humanitarian organization of the Catholic community in the United States. I had missed the committee's first conference call and was eager to catch up with Bishop Thomas on what had transpired at their meeting.

The mission of CRS, which was founded by the United States Conference of Catholic Bishops, is to act on the good news of the Gospel by serving the poorest and most vulnerable people in the world on the basis of need, and not creed. It operates in approximately one hundred countries and reaches out to 100 million people. Its programs include humanitarian relief, food aid, health, water, sanitation, education, livelihood, and peace-building. My six years on the board had opened my eyes to the suffering in the world and the effective solutions brought about by the deeply committed CRS staff.

I reached Bishop Thomas in his car with his mother on their way to join family for Thanksgiving. We exchanged courtesies, and then I asked my question about the committee meeting. "Well," Bishop Thomas replied, "we were actually glad you were absent because we talked about you. We would like you to be a candidate for the position."

I don't know whether I laughed out loud, but I know I laughed inside. "You must be kidding," I said. "I have no depth in international development." Honestly, I could not then name all the countries in Africa, nor the capitals of those I did know, and definitely not the political, ethnic, religious, cultural, or economic complexities of the countries where CRS worked.

"Now, Bishop Thomas, you know as much about international relief and development as I do. What would you do if the committee asked you to be a candidate?" I asked in a joking way. His answer changed my life: "I would get down on my knees and pray."

Bishop Thomas was serious. He made clear this was not an offer, that other candidates would be considered, some working for CRS.

"You would be rigorously reviewed in the same way that every candidate would be. We are asking you to be open, to not say 'no' at this point, to let the process unfold and let the Holy Spirit guide you. Could you do that for us?"

I promised an answer after the long holiday weekend.

Thanksgiving is one of my favorite celebrations, truly a time of giving thanks, of acknowledging how much God has blessed us by giving us each other. My husband David and our two sons, Ryan (then twenty-six and a third-year medical student) and Justin (twenty-three and a graduate student in theology), do little other than eat and relax. We hang out together, take in a few movies and set our minds toward Advent and Christmas. I thought that this period of calm and the heightened awareness of love and blessings would be a good time to pray and give Bishop Thomas's question its proper attention.

My assumption was that I could not be and should not be the person to fill this position. I knew enough to know what I didn't know, and I did not think the well-being and lives of CRS beneficiaries should be in my hands.

Beyond the reports presented at board meetings and the trips I had taken to learn about CRS programming in various countries — India, Sri Lanka, Indonesia, Kenya, Ethiopia, Pakistan, Afghanistan — I had absolutely no formal education or experience in this highly complex field.

Each sector of work and each country CRS serves must fill tomes of analysis, engage the study and imagination of thousands of experts, and constitute the work of numerous government and nonprofit institutions. Emergencies call for quick decisions and incisive actions. It was clear to me that I had little to offer and would not be a value-added proposition.

Saying "yes" to a candidacy is different from saying "yes" to a job. But even doing that was hard. Because I am of Chinese ancestry and a woman, I am often asked to be a candidate in searches — there are significant pressures on committees and consultants to include minority and female candidates in all searches, particularly for executive officer positions. Some good has resulted from this requirement as we have seen more qualified candidates from nontraditional pools gain visibility and consideration. I support this. However, I do not consent to letting myself be placed on such lists.

Saying "yes" would also open me up to the possibility of making the type of move I had undertaken only twice up to that point in my life — first when I left Hong Kong for the United States in 1972, and second when I left Purdue University after twenty-three years to come to Notre Dame. That had been over fourteen years ago.

I don't move around a lot. I flourish in communities where there are deep relationships. At Purdue and Notre Dame, I always felt that the next best thing was not something or someplace else, but just the next day of work with the people and for the mission I had chosen to serve. Leaving Purdue for Notre Dame took a full year of grieving. Once that was over, I was sure the campus in South Bend, Indiana, was where God intended me to spend the rest of my career, the rest of my life. David and I had already purchased a lot for our final resting place in Cedar Grove, the cemetery in the middle of campus. This was not macabre for the Notre Dame community: it is a privilege many people seek.

So, it would not be right for me to be on the candidate list: it would be a false representation of my interest, and it could hold back the search committee's effort to identify truly viable diversity candidates. But I felt that I owed CRS and the committee the obedience they asked of me, to not say "no." In my years on the board, I had come to love CRS, and I had the utmost respect and affection for the individuals on the committee. It was hard to refuse them.

That brought up another issue. Even though I knew I would not qualify and did not think the committee would seriously consider me, it would be humbling to be turned down. I also knew that such information, as much as it is meant to be confidential, would be known by others. So not only would I fail, I would fail with people knowing! I could devote a whole book to the concept of "losing face" in the Chinese culture, but suffice it to say that the combination of pride and the fear of embarrassment was enough to make me recoil from the thought of undergoing an evaluation only to be found deficient.

It was pride, and I knew what to do about that: pray, pray, pray, and pray. Pray to the point where I can say: it is okay, I can handle this; this is a short embarrassment, and I will get over it in days. I may feel flushed in my face; I may be down for a day, but I can handle this. Besides, it is good at my age, no longer at the point where people's opinion should matter, to eat humble pie. My friends would be there for me. So I can take this on for Bishop Thomas and CRS.

Peace achieved: I gave my answer to Bishop Thomas the next week. Yes, I would be a candidate.

CHAPTER TWO

"... Not Pros and Cons, but Joy and Fears"

That was the first step on the road that had eventually brought me here to Cambodia. I was accompanied on this trip by Catholic Relief Services Board Chair Bishop Gerry Kicanas of Tucson, Mundelein faculty member Fr. Gus Belaskus, and various CRS colleagues. The occasion was the twenty-fifth anniversary of CRS's work in the country. CRS had been here from 1973 to 1975, helping victims of the brutal war. We returned in 1992 after the signing of the Paris Peace Accords that ended the war with Vietnam and brought stability back to the country.

Tuol Slang is only one of the four hundred mass graves in Cambodia from the days of the Killing Fields in the 1970s, when the entire Cambodian society was stripped of its worth and dignity, when the aspects of life we most cherish — faith, education, marriage, family — were denigrated. Around the trunk of one tree and on fences circling the graves were a multitude of colorful string bracelets. They belonged to the children who perished. In the circles of red, yellow, blue, and green, one could see childhood joys, simple pleasures, innocence.

Respectfully removing our shoes, we entered a glass tower that holds the skulls, bones, and ragged clothing of those killed. There was a depth of sadness, not only for the massacred, but also for the brutality that humans are capable of. I felt that I was standing on sacred ground. My lips formed a prayer. All I could think was, "Why, God?"

Later, I attended a dinner celebrating CRS's work in Cambodia. I sat with the leaders of ministries and agencies that work with us to improve education, health, and livelihoods. They exuded energy, poise, and intelligence. How could that be with those killing fields so close by, in geography and in time?

The man on my right had attended Oxford, a bit older than his fellow students due to years spent in the countryside under the Khmer Rouge. On my left was an attractive and vivacious lady who had trained to become a physician in France. Next to her was a man who went to Minneapolis and Boston to earn degrees in public health.

They certainly had different backgrounds, but they told me that under the Pol Pot regime they began each day hungry, wondering where they would find food. But they also talked about their education, careers, families, and the difficulty in balancing work and children — these were the kind of conversations I was used to having at Notre Dame with bright young people eager to go out and make their marks on the world. I had grown accustomed to hearing what I heard that evening — laughter, a celebration of spirit, drive, opportunities, caring.

I loved my students at Notre Dame. Even as I submitted my curriculum vitae and references to the CRS search committee, I knew that I was not looking for a change in my career. I thought, indeed was hoping, that in a few months they would find other strong candidates, and I would be thanked, and that would be the end of it.

I had been working hard for many years, really for my whole life. David and I were ready to slow down a bit with the boys grown and our careers at a comfortable place. It seemed like a time for harvest after all the years of planting. Things could not have been better for me at Notre Dame. In my third term as dean of the Mendoza College of Business, the undergraduate business program had achieved top placement — for two years in a row — in the highly visible *Bloomberg-BusinessWeek* ranking. (The Mendoza College continues to hold this top position to the time of this writing.) The graduate programs had also moved into the tier of top schools, and enrollment across all the programs exceeded our goals.

The CRS search process moved ahead. There was an in-depth interview with a consultant from a national executive search firm. My hoped-for quick dismissal from the list of candidates did not happen. The consultant told me that my expertise in strategy and change management made up for my lack of knowledge of overseas development work. My Ph.D. in business focuses on strategic management, a discipline that addresses why, when confronted with change, some organizations adapt and flourish while others go the way of the dinosaurs.

Strategic management was a nascent field when I was drawn to it in the mid-1970s, but since 1975 I had studied, researched, taught, consulted on, and practiced strategic analysis and implementation. It is now second nature to me to observe organizations, both profit and nonprofit, in terms of their state of well-being and the underlying factors that contribute to that. A doctor automatically notices if someone is flushed, laboring in his breathing, or showing signs of pain, and starts to run through diagnoses in her head. This is similar to what I do when observing an organization.

CRS possessed deep expertise in international development, but not as much in strategic management and organizational development. And internal CRS studies indicated that change was ahead. Significant shifts in the aid environment could adversely affect resources even as they raised expectations from both donors and beneficiaries. Innovation and greater accountability would be necessary.

I recognized these patterns. Raising the game in an incremental fashion would not be sufficient. Successful alignment with the future requires objective detachment from what has worked in the past, the current core activities and skills of the staff, as well as the existing priorities for resource allocation.

CRS is deeply committed to serving the poorest and most vulnerable, but I knew passion and commitment were not sufficient. Its desire to work for the common good must be accompanied by uncommon excellence that achieves demonstrable, sustainable, and holistic improvements for individuals, families, and communities. To keep walking down the same path would actually increase the risk to the agency.

I was beginning to realize that perhaps my three decades of work in strategy might be something CRS needed. For the first time since November, I understood that I was not just a token for the search, but perhaps I had a contribution to make. In any case, I felt a responsibility to ensure that these issues were brought to the surface, understood, and acted upon. I did not know where this would lead other than to the knot I had in my stomach: I might have to face the question about leaving Notre Dame.

That was going to be very tough to do. Everything was so right here, all in place. Why would God call on me to disrupt that? Dave and I loved our community, particularly the priests and sisters of the Congregation of Holy Cross, who have become our family over the last fourteen years. Equally daunting was the idea of giving up tenure. Even with the ongoing evaluations in a person's career, tenure is the biggest hurdle for an academic. When faculty members come up for tenure, usually in the sixth year of employment, they go through a rigorous, some think blistering, process of review by both internal and external colleagues. Those who fail to achieve tenure leave. Success, on the other hand, brings lifelong employment with dismissal only for egregious behavior and utter incompetence. When I went through the tenure process, it was the only time that I broke into hives. Most people never give up tenure once they've earned it. This was almost unthinkable for me, an immigrant, to whom security is the brass ring.

Though the thought of leaving Notre Dame was emotionally wrenching, I felt that if I were to allow myself to stay in the search, I needed to be willing to consider this possibility. Otherwise it would be disingenuous and a waste of everyone's time.

I turned to Fr. Ken Molinaro, C.S.C., for spiritual direction. I had served with Fr. Ken on a committee and had gotten to know him. Fr. Ken gets up every morning at 4:30 to pray, and I can see his calm, kindness, and surrender to God in everything he does. There were others I could have turned to, but they were my closest friends and would be conflicted as I was. At our first counseling session, I told Fr. Ken that I had tried to think this through, to list the pros and cons, to make a decision tree, but these had not been helpful at all. I would like his help. His reply: "Carolyn, you are by nature an analytical thinker, but thinking will not give you the answer."

Fr. Ken was spot on in his reading of me. I am indeed a highly analytical person. Whenever I encounter a situation, I study it, note the benefits and costs, the downside risk and the upside gain, the value for the investments whether these are financial or human efforts, the quantifiable and qualitative, sunk costs and opportunity costs. In many ways, these approaches have served me well by fostering objectivity, logic, discipline, clarity, and accountability.

But I have learned that a few things do not lend themselves to this calculus; and looking back, they are inevitably matters of the heart: a call for action that amounts to a leap into a big "unknown," leaving behind what is safe and perfect to answer a question that will not go away.

The two similar moves I had made — leaving Hong Kong and leaving Purdue — were wrenching because I was leaving my homes, my communities, my cocoons. I had grown and flourished in both communities and had developed deep roots of friendship and love. As I have said, departure from each drew a year of grieving. I was at that juncture again.

Instead of pros and cons, Fr. Ken directed me to joys and fears: these are the language of the heart. Better still, I did not have to labor at it; I just had to carry a piece of paper and jot down my thoughts and emotions when they came. I would maintain my regular prayer routine and offer up my questions to God. God would speak. Well, this seemed manageable, and I constructed my mental to-do list: (1) pray for guidance, (2) have paper with me, and (3) record thoughts and emotions.

CHAPTER THREE

The Fears Came First

It seemed easy, but what came first were the fears. In full force, they took up the invitation to speak to me and had lots to say. Night sweats would wake me up at 3 a.m., unusual for me. Not much wakes me up, but, like Ebenezer Scrooge, I had three rounds of middle-of-the-night visitors, each with a specific concern and each lasting for two to three weeks.

Fear of Incompetence

The first round had me worrying about leading in a field where I have not only minimal knowledge but the *least* knowledge among all my colleagues. I dreamt about show-ing up at meetings having prepared the wrong material, running out of time to read everything, or trying to speak but no words would come. I woke up to a sense of panic and embarrassment. Following Fr. Ken's instructions, I would write down these fears on the pad I kept on the night table next to my bed, acknowledge my fear, give this to God, and fall back to sleep.

Depth of knowledge is the calling card for academics and the basis of legitimacy for our credibility. Academics draw very tight perimeters within which they will plumb deep. One has to be clear on which microslice of what topic one is proffering unassailable knowledge and opinion. Be-cause they often interact with others who have equivalent depth but on different topics, academics are very careful not to wander into areas (even highly related contiguous topics) that are not their specializations. There is no word more damning to an academic than "shallow." Thus the idea of leading an organization when I possessed little knowledge horrified me.

During the day, I actually did not think about it. Fr. Ken's instruction freed me from having to resolve the problem: I was merely to listen, to note, to name my fear. There was no analytic with which to approach this, I would just offer it to God. Somehow, in random moments, insights would come, and they would help me move past a hurdle.

I cannot tell you when these insights arrived or where they came from — it was almost like a doorbell rang and a message was delivered. Out of the blue, it dawned on me that I had never presented myself as an international development specialist; nothing on my résumé would indicate that. I had not misled anyone. Given that the search committee could not have seen international development on my résumé, they must be looking for something else.

At that point, I recalled the words of a beloved mentor who had since passed away. Dr. Robert Ringel, Executive Vice President of Academic Affairs (EVPAA) — essentially the provost — of Purdue University, had offered me the position of Associate EVPAA. At that time, I had had only one semester as a full professor and felt completely unqualified and unprepared for the position. I had no exposure to university governance and budgets, nor had I been engaged in the deliberation of decisions for which the Office of the EVPAA would develop policy guidance.

Even though the post of Associate EVPAA would be several steps up the hierarchy, I did not think it was time for me to move on to a new assignment. I turned down Dr.

Ringel and the assignment. To show proper respect in the Chinese way, my letter presented a litany of the many things I had not handled and areas for which I had no expertise. I highlighted my deficiencies and concluded that he deserved someone better and more knowledgeable than me.

That evening I ran into Dr. Ringel at the intermission of a concert. He was disappointed and somber. He told me that he was not capable of small talk because he just lost a friend to suicide, so he would speak directly, perhaps undiplomatically. He then said three things to I.

First, I should not put myself down and focus on things I had not done. What we do not know in the universe is unbounded. Humility does not require us to deny or diminish what we have done, what we have invested to learn, and the contributions we stand to make.

Second, he noted that I should trust him: he knew what I had and had not done; he could decipher my strengths, gaps, and experiences.

Third, and most important, he knew what he needed. He felt that I had not given any weight to his judgment in reaching out to me. He was right. He told me to call him when I felt ready to move on, that he would have a place for me on his team.

In the winter of 2011, when I was overwhelmed by what I did not know about international development, Dr. Ringel's words from 1993 came flooding into my memory. Were he alive, he would be one of the first persons I would call. Though he was gone, he still spoke to me. When I did join the Purdue EVPAA Office two years after our talk, I did not end up crafting administrative policies, but assumed the responsibility for designing and coordinating the university-wide strategic planning, change management, and continuous improvement processes. My role was unique to the university, was complementary to others' efforts, and drew on expertise I had developed over decades.

Such insights settled my nerves and helped me turn my focus to what I could do rather than what I could not do. Just as important was the acknowledgment that CRS, with five thousand employees, easily enjoys more than fifty thousand people-years of knowledge about international development. If I were to become CRS's CEO, I would need to respect what I did not know and turn to and access the deep expertise of colleagues. I found the opportunity for others to help me lead energizing. I have taught executive leadership for a long time, and one of the myths and blind spots is that the leader should know everything and make every decision. This is unhealthy for the leader and grossly underutilizes the talents within the organization. In some ways, having decades of experience may get in the way of cultivating others' perspectives and developing their leadership potential.

My fear about incompetence lost its grip on me.

Fear of Danger

My second round of night sweats brought into consciousness the danger of being in highly insecure countries and also the fear that something might happen to David while I am gone on one of my many trips. Among the countries in which CRS serves, many face a high degree of violence or are exposed to health and physical hazards. Threats to personnel in the development sector have been rising steadily over the years.

I was in Ethiopia as a CRS board member in 2008. We arrived at our hotel one hour after a bomb exploded in a minibus across the street. We were fortunate in that our arrival was held up because of a delay in baggage handling. In 2010, I spent five days in Afghanistan when three security threats took place: the first targeted the staff of another humanitarian organization; the second was an explosion that sprayed shrapnel and injured the wife of a CRS staff member; and the third incident involved a round of attacks near the airport from which I would be leaving later that afternoon. My middle-of-the-night thoughts drifted to Fr. Larry Jenco, who was kidnapped in Lebanon in 1985 by members of the radical group Islamic Holy War and released after 564 days in captivity. At that time, he was serving as CRS Lebanon country manager.

It should be noted that CRS has very strict security protocols that include comprehensive training, restrictions in movements, readiness preparation, ratings of countries for the assignment of personnel, as well as participation in various networks for security updates and evacuations. Safety is the number-one concern, and all decisions pivot around this. Yet unpredictable violence is always a part of some of our operating environments.

And the risks are not confined to man-made violence. When I went to Indonesia in 2005 to survey the tsunami relief, an aftershock brought on an earthquake of 8.7 on the Richter scale while I was on the top — eighth — floor of a hotel. All these were on my mind as I sat up in bed in the middle of the night. I felt strongly that as CEO one should be ready to go wherever the staff are; otherwise we have no business putting people there. Did I have the courage? Could I embrace this aspect of the position?

A bigger worry was about my husband. Dave is relatively healthy but has had blackouts due to atrial fibrillation, which causes an irregular heartbeat. What would happen if David had a blackout and I was not there?

This fear is essentially about death. That is, of course, a big one. I had no answers: I just gave this to God. As in the first round of worries, insights would just come: sometimes in church, and more often in the cafés where I tended to do my work. A thought came to me amidst coffee and a pile of work that I was not with David either of the times he had his spells. One time, a friend was there; the other time Dave was alone. As it was, I travelled a lot as dean. Right around that time, someone told me the story of a man who went down to the basement to get a bottle of wine and had a fatal heart attack. It dawned on me that things could happen any time, in or out of my presence, regardless of where I worked. The key is to trust God, to know that David is in His care as much as in mine.

We should always be prudent, sensible, and responsible. I am not the risk-seeker type: chasing storms, bungee jumping, and extreme sports hold absolutely no thrill for me. But it was also clear that we can allow the worry about death to clutch us so tightly that we give up living. We take risks daily, every time we cross a street or get in a car. I had to trust my CRS colleagues: if they designate a country or region as sufficiently safe for operations, then it will be safe enough for me. The big question really is: do we trust that God is always with us? That we are in the palm of His hand?

There was a final message that came to me. While death is loss and loss is painful, our Christian faith tells us that death is not a punishment. It is the return to the Father who made us and to the home where each of us was promised a place. It is life continued in a different form, where we finally know love for all that it is and not through a mirror dimly. Whatever loss there is, eventually we will be together again. Another mentor for me is Fr. Theodore "Ted" Hesburgh, C.S.C., the legendary President Emeritus of the University of Notre Dame. When he spoke of death during a homily, his eyes sparkled, and he recited the verse "Eye has not seen, and ear has not heard … what God has prepared for those who love him" (1 Corinthians 2:9). How long we are meant to be on this earth is God's call, not ours. I was able to put the fear of mishaps for Dave and me in God's hands and felt a sense of relief.

Fear of Change

The third set of worries that woke me up was kind of silly: a leap from the sublime to the mundane. I am a creature of habit, and I do not like to spend a lot of time attending to daily logistics. I keep the same doctors, dentist, dry cleaner, beauty salon, seamstress, fitness club, shoe repair, car maintenance, grocery store, and Chinese supply store. I am also not a great driver and have a poor sense of direction. Navigating in new cities is always Dave's job. A new location would require me to start all over again. By then, we had also decided that if I were to be offered the job at CRS, David would stay in South Bend. It wouldn't make sense for him to move to Baltimore with me because I would be traveling so much. So I would be on my own quite a bit.

I woke up tied in knots over the most trivial matters. Should I move my car to Baltimore or keep it in South Bend? Where will I take my dry-cleaning? Where will I exercise? Should we drive back and forth or spend the money flying back and forth to South Bend? Who will cut my hair? Where will I take my clothes for alterations? I felt like Gulliver as each strand of his hair was pinned down by his tiny captors until he was immobilized.

In the daylight, I recognized these concerns for what they were: about change, about giving up what is familiar, about meeting new challenges, and about leaving one's community. I felt an attachment to the people behind those services. These individuals — like Karen who did my alterations, Laura who cut my hair, the Sisters of Holy Cross who welcome us every Sunday to worship with them, our faith-filled and gracious neighbors John and Jan Jenkins, my colleagues at the Mendoza College — are friends who care for each other. I did not want to let them go.

Leaving would be hard, as I knew only too well from experience. For me, it would be akin to removing old contact paper from drawers. When the glue of the liner has bonded with the wood fiber of the drawer, the paper does not come off easily and jagged pieces remain.

As I dealt with this, one word from Jesus was lodged in my head: "Go." It seemed that every reading in scripture at that time echoed that invitation: Abraham, Moses, Isaiah, Jonah, the disciples, St. Paul, and so on. "Go" — a simple enough word; I got the message.

Then there was another word — joy.

CHAPTER FOUR

Joy: A Journey

Joy did not come through night visitors, nor did it seize me with exuberant song and dance. It came from a sense that God may be calling, that He had been leading me on a journey where the past revealed its purpose in a specific invitation for the future. I did not grow up in a particularly religious family and would not consider myself to have good prayer and spiritual habits. Yet in my earlier departures from Hong Kong and Purdue, I was moved by some force bigger than myself for reasons that logic cannot explain. And, in hindsight, I saw how every step in my journey led to where I stood that day and was enveloped by the grace and the blessings of these experiences.

My Parents, Peter Woo (aka Ching Chi)
and Hung U-Lan

I was born on April 19, 1954, in Hong Kong, in the neighborhood known as "Happy Valley," which got its name from the iconic horse race course built there in 1846. My Western name, "Carolyn," was chosen by my father. My Chinese name is Woo Yau Yan (吳幼仁), with "吳" (Woo) as our family name. "幼" (Yau) is the character for "delicate," which comes from my mother's given name, and "仁" (Yan) is the character given to all the girls in my family. This character represents the Confucian teaching on how people should relate to one another.

I was the fifth child of my parents, Peter Woo and Hung U-Lan. More importantly, I was the fourth daughter who arrived when my parents were hoping for their second son. My father wanted two sons for "an heir and a spare." There was talk that if the fifth child were not a son, my father would consider taking a second wife — legal at the time. Both my maternal and paternal grandfathers had multiple wives. And that was a possibility as this fourth girl arrived, much to my father's chagrin. Fortunately my mother conceived fairly quickly afterward, and my younger brother arrived twenty months later. In a twelve-year span, my parents had six children: Helen, Paul, Irene, Maureen, me, and William.

My parents' personalities and backgrounds could hardly have been more different. My father was born around 1916 in China. As an infant, he was purchased by the third wife of a man who would technically be my paternal grandfather. My father didn't talk much about his family as he had very little memory of his early years, and I don't think he ever felt like he belonged. As a boy, he was sent away to St. Joseph's boarding school in Hong Kong. It was there he became Catholic. My father was sent for university studies in Germany but enjoyed himself too much to master German, so he transferred to schools in Scotland and received a degree from the Royal Technical College in Glasgow in architecture. The plan was for him to serve the family shipping business located in southern China.

Peter Woo was smart, urbane, daring, and had little experience of family structure. He had always been on his own, made all his own decisions, and did things on his own terms. He loved dancing, bridge, drinking, and probably

European dames, as he gave Irish names to all his daughters. In the midst of World War II, he returned to Hong Kong and started work as a naval architect: a profession in strong demand given that Hong Kong's most distinctive asset is its harbor. My father apparently enjoyed his life as a bachelor in this British colony with his Western flair and full command of the English language. Two incidents, however, disrupted his life: one, he was introduced to my mother; and two, he was summoned by the Japanese, who by then were occupying Hong Kong, to serve its naval interests. For a Chinese man, that would be an act of treason.

While my father grew up on his own, my mother was a hothouse flower protected from all the challenges of life. She was also from China, the only natural child of the first wife of my grandfather, who came from a wealthy family and was known for his generosity. His favorite child was my mother, who, for as long as she could remember, had her own maids and servant girls. The family sought temporary refuge in Hong Kong when China fell to the Japanese.

My mother was named Hung U-Lan (delicate orchid). Tutors came to the home — she never had to go to a school, take an exam, cope with due dates, or face pressures from anything related to school. The learning regimen was constructed around her comfort level. My mother learned the proper manners befitting a young lady, developed an exquisite taste for fabrics, and was renowned for her tailoring abilities. The Chinese did not have access to Butterick or Simplicity patterns, so my mother learned to cut fabric without a pattern to make any clothing item we needed. It is a skill I never picked up.

We always thought that my mother was four years younger than my father until, after her death, we learned the long-held secret: they were the same age. For her generation,

my mother married late because, the story goes, my grandmother did not find any young man worthy until she met
my father. Since Chinese marriages in those days were primarily engineered by parents, my grandmother's approval
was paramount. While my grandmother was brought up in
the "old" Chinese way, when foot-binding was the practice,
she preferred a more modern approach and did not put my
mother through that torture. She liked my father's Western
ways and the possibility of a different type of marriage for
my mother.

We think our mother was smitten also. After a few
dates, all chaperoned, the question of marriage came up.
Like my father, my mother also faced a problem with the
occupiers. The family had received an inquiry from a Japanese military officer for the hand of my mother. The only
acceptable (though not truthful) answer they could give:
she was already engaged.

So Peter Woo and Hung U-Lan, who were as different
as night and day and who hardly knew each other, married
on September 21, 1943. They immediately fled to China,
where some regions were under Japanese occupation and
other areas were fighting to retain control. As for so many,
the war years were very difficult. My father could not work.
My parents had to stay a step ahead of the Japanese, sometimes literally fleeing late at night on foot. My older siblings
Helen and Paul were born during this period. My mother
was resourceful and strong in ways she never had to be before. To generate cash, she gave her jewelry to my father to
sell on the street. She would recount the agreement among
fellow travelers on the run from the Japanese that the safety
of the group could not be compromised by crying babies.

Years later, I got a glimpse of the trauma when I went
to the movie *Tora! Tora! Tora!* with my mother. She sobbed

from the beginning to the end: her whole life was upended by the invasion of the Japanese. The world she knew and grew up in disappeared in the war. Though we heard many stories of danger, escape, hardships, and bravery, I wish that we had heard and asked more about the bond that my parents developed as a newly married couple completely on their own in that chaotic, dangerous world. For example, I inherited a beautiful diamond and pearl gold bangle from my mother that my father bought from another peddler when he should have been selling, not buying, jewelry. I cherish this as part of the love story of my parents. I now know that we should ask, probe, dig deep to get our parents' love story because this is a source of the magic of our lives.

The Immigrant Life

After the war, my parents returned to Hong Kong. It was supposed to be only temporary. They were planning to re-settle in China. But a trip back to Fujien, their home province, sensitized them to another looming event: the onset of the Communist revolution. If my parents thought that their lives would return to normal after World War II, their plans were crushed.

In China, leaving one's home meant leaving one's assets and security, as land was the primary currency of wealth. Land was not just a financial holding, it was also part of one's birthright, identity, and ancestry. Giving it up means an abrupt severing of the bond to one's past.

I got some idea of what this meant when, in the 1990s, I brought my mother back to her childhood home in Xia-men, a large city in Fujien. The few remaining carved wood panels in the courtyard bore some indications of the home's former elegance, but different sections and gardens of the home had been destroyed, torn down to make room for a factory, or carved up into one-room apartments. She tried to picture for me not only what the house once looked like, but also the warm glow of family and festivities that took place in that estate.

I also recall the night in the 1960s when my father received a telegram from China informing him of the removal of the ancestral graves from his home. He put down the letter, took off his spectacles, wiped away his tears, and could not speak.

The experiences of displacement by war and revolutions — starting all over again, figuring out how to make a living, finding one's place in a new society — are very much the story of the immigrants, like my parents, who populated Hong Kong while I was growing up. Some would find their footing and make meaningful progress along a steady track. But others never adjusted to their new position, never found their place in their world's new order.

Displacement was a common theme of my formative years. My mother, in a society with a new language and new technologies, was like an orchid that lost the protection of the greenhouse. Relatives from China took up temporary residence on our couches on their way to new lives. In the years of the Cultural Revolution in China, some told stories of the brutality of the Red Guards.

And of course, we were all keenly aware that Hong Kong's status under the British would come to an end in 1997, when the colony would revert to Communist rule. What my parents had faced, political turmoil and regime change, would also be the defining reality for my generation. The hidden gift in this situation for my peers and me was that we seldom wasted time or resisted change. Everyone was focused on creating options and opportunities.

Change would come, and it was just a matter of how we would prepare for it. In light of this background, it's not surprising that leading organizations through change would eventually be my profession.

Given my father's disappointment at not getting a son when I was born, one would imagine that we would not be close. It was the opposite. I credit this to the ingenuity of my nanny, whom we called Gaga long before there was Lady Gaga. My care was entrusted to her. Every morning I would join my father for breakfast. I was seated at a little table at his side — as children, we did not ascend to the "big" table until we learned our manners. My father would share his eggs and sausage with me. We had a chauffeur who drove my dad to work, and after breakfast my nanny would pack me up to go on the ride with him.

Schools in Hong Kong were so crowded with the swell of immigrant children that grades one, three, and five would get the afternoon shift, while two, four, and six went in the morning. So when I was in first and third grade, I got to ride with my father on his way to work. Even then, he was very proud of my good grades and showered me with admiration for my excellence in work and studies. I remember vividly that in third grade, during one of our rides, I told him that one day I would be a professor with a doctorate. I have no idea where that came from. Perhaps my father was reading one of his favorite magazines and mentioned with admiration some accomplished scholar with a Ph.D. I just automatically declared that, of course, this is what I would become.

My academic drive also provided me with a sense of belonging and worth. As the fifth child — and especially the fourth daughter with a younger brother — I was sort of lost in the shuffle. My two older sisters Irene and Maureen were pretty, while I was a chubby child. Friends of the family would affectionately describe me as "taking after my dad," when everyone noted that my sisters resembled my mom, a lovely woman. Academic achievement became a safe haven for me, a place where nothing could go wrong, a solution to every challenge and worry. My drive was intense; it came from a place of insecurity and was a way to earn my worth. I was also compensating for my sister and brother who would upset my father with their terrible grades and embarrass my mother at teachers' conferences.

Ah Gaga, My Nanny

My nanny did more than solidify my relationship with my father — she basically took care of me, becoming one of the most important people in my life. Though the arrival of my younger brother precluded my father's taking another wife, my parents' marriage was still difficult for my mother. In a traditional Chinese marriage, wives are completely dependent on their husbands. They were given an allowance and not much decision-making power. Men were not always faithful to their wives. And, of course, polygamy was still legal and an acceptable cultural practice. Women were talked down to and seldom treated as equals. Most Chinese mothers passed this attitude on: sons were the sun and moon, the hope and anchor for their old age. Daughters, not so much.

While there were moments of tenderness in my parents' marriage, it also had its share of quarrels. My father tended to leave home after dinner and return in the wee hours of the morning. My mother took to staying up late and seldom went to bed before 2 a.m. Her nocturnal routine left little time for us to interact. Sometimes when I was in high school, when I pulled all-nighters for exams, we would share her midnight snacks of soup and noodles. But when I was young, I felt that my mother only managed to give me her leftover energy. Years later, I would understand that my mother was in a hard place herself; that it was difficult coping with all the changes she had faced in her life. My father's behavior also created many deep hurts.

My nanny's full name is Fung Yau (馮友), with 馮 "Fung" as the family name and 友 "Yau" as the given name meaning "friend." While it is pronounced the same as the "Yau" in my name, they represent different Chinese characters. She joined our family eight years before I was born and still lives in Hong Kong today. For some reason, one of my sisters called her Gaga, or Ah Gaga because in the Cantonese dialect a reference to someone is often preceded with "ah." Gaga has been part of our family for four generations, from my grandparents to our children.

Gaga was the eldest daughter of four children born to a farmer-scholar in the Kwongtung province around 1918. When her father died of tuberculosis, which was not unusual in those days, Gaga became a servant girl. She was eleven years old, making fifty Chinese cents a month. The entire sum was given to her mother for raising her younger siblings. As the maid for the young children of her employer, she carried their bags when they went to the village school. Gaga learned how to read by standing outside the classroom and listening to the lessons, gaining sufficient mastery to read the newspaper, although she never had the opportunity to learn to write.

The family that employed her was kind to her and taught her great manners. When World War II broke out in China, the family moved to Saigon and took her with them. In that French colony, she developed a love for French amenities and Shirley Temple movies. One of her treats was the

French perfume Night of Paris. She never wore it herself, but she would put a dab into my hair after she finished braiding it. Gaga was known for her beauty accentuated by a poise that was almost regal.

Several times, her employers wanted to arrange a marriage for her. The intended grooms were other house servants or heavy laborers. My nanny turned down every attempt. In those days, it was unthinkable for a Chinese woman to reject marriage, but Gaga felt that her first duty was to her mother and siblings, who counted on her wages. Marriage would jeopardize her ability to continue working and directing all her resources to her family. Her independence was important to her, and she would rather work hard on her own terms than enter into a marriage where she would completely depend on the whims, kindness, generosity, or small-mindedness of a husband. After the war, she decided to move from Saigon to Hong Kong, where opportunities would be more plentiful and she would be closer to China.

In 1946, Fung Yau was hired as a servant to help my mother take care of my sister Irene. When I was born, we became inseparable. To get me out of the way of the adults, she carried me on her back using a Chinese-style Snugli while she conducted her chores of cleaning and laundering. She and I (and at certain times different siblings) shared the same room all the time I was growing up. It was to her I would spill out my worries — when my parents quarreled or, later, when my father had his first heart attack. I would complain to her about the privileged place my brothers enjoyed. Together we processed the news on the late-night radio show that reported the murder of a popular Hong Kong journalist when he spoke out against Communism. One of my earliest memories is from the time Gaga took ill when I was only three. I brought a stool and sat at the foot of her bed, watching over her until she opened her eyes and was well again.

Every morning when Ah Gaga got me ready for kindergarten at the Precious Blood School, she would send me off with perfect braids, the whitest starched uniform, matching spotless white socks and shoes, and a little wet towel in a soap box. In those days, the teacher would stamp in the student record book a "rabbit" for good behavior (attentiveness, neat appearance, completion of homework, obedient conduct) and a "pig" for anything less. Before I left for school each morning, my nanny would say to me that she had done her part in getting me ready and that I should do my part to bring home a rabbit for the day. I was glad to do that because the rabbit would be for both of us. After a year of only rabbits on my record book, I won a gold medal. Carved on it were my name and the Chinese characters for perfect conduct. It was placed on a chain for me to wear. I bit on it regularly, and it was so thin and pliable that I left little teeth marks. To this day it is one of my most cherished possessions.

Through the years, my nanny continued to instill in me a strong sense of discipline and the willingness to work hard. I did my homework in the same room where she ironed. She was a perfectionist in all she did. Her commandment — "Don't play until you finish your work" — is forever chiseled into my brain. When I whimpered about the quantity of work, I only had to look at her duties and knew I could do more. At sixteen, when I took a practice test for the SAT and scored miserably on the verbal section, I was crestfallen. When I told Gaga that I did not know enough English words, she suggested, in the most pragmatic fashion, that I spend an extra hour a night studying the dictionary. I did and got over the hump.

Despite her long hours, my nanny saw work as a privilege. Work was worthwhile because it allowed her to contribute to the well-being of others: the Woo family; her mother and siblings; her eleven nieces; and the families of her coworkers. There was an aesthetic that came from work done well: spotless laundry; a perfect crease; a shiny floor. It was my nanny's way of showing respect for the duties she was given and living up to the expectation she held for herself.

For a person who has so little by the standards of the world, Ah Gaga exuded an immense sense of gratitude. Every morning, her first act upon rising was to light two sticks of incense, clasp these in her hands, kneel down on the kitchen floor in front of the window, and bow deeply. It was her way to thank the heavens and the earth. Even today in assisted living, gratitude overflows from her every gesture. Though she did not convert to Catholicism until her nineties, Gaga would be the one who dusted the framed portrait of the Blessed Mother hung in the dining room in our house and picked fresh flowers from my mother's roof garden to honor her. When she was worried about us, she would pray to the Blessed Mother. When we were rude or did stupid things, she would remind us that the Blessed Mother sees all and knows all. We would have to answer to her.

This spirituality also engendered a strong ethical sense that led her to speak the truth, stand up for what is right, and protect the weak. Gaga was deeply loyal to our family. She got many offers involving less work and more money, but turned all of them down to be with us, particularly when the going was tough. Through the years our relatives and friends would come to regard her with great affection and respect. When my father was being taken to the hospital for the last time, Gaga rode in the ambulance with him. It was to this humble servant that he spoke of his regrets and gave her the mandate to take care of his wife and children. After my mother passed away in 2000, I went through a ceremony in the presence of my siblings, kneeling and offering tea to Gaga to make her my "adopted mother." She would be servant no more. In Gaga — Fung Yau's — honor I gave my older son the Chinese name "Yau Yee," meaning friendship. And I sometimes wear a pin with her name, 友 (Yau), in her honor.

My nanny also made it possible for me to look at the world from the standpoint of a servant without power, money, or prestige. I see her in the people who have no options and access to education; I see her in the children who have lost their parents and are on their own; I see her in those who look in from the outside. It is not lost on me that my strength and eventual success were first formed by a person of very humble background. In our work, CRS encounters the poor who sell one child to feed another; orphans who become heads of households when their parents die of AIDS; refugees; disabled; people with no place at the table. My work would be a chance to repay a debt.

My strong belief that God is present to us through people first came to me through the gift of Gaga. She formed me in important ways: work habits; discipline; and values. But she made the Christian teachings I learned at school real: she made love and devotion real; she demonstrated the power of a life guided by the spirit; she saw the needs of others and gave everything she had. I was not just an observer of this love; I was its beneficiary. It means I can never deny the capacity we have for each other. The people who love us open us to experience God.

Looking at that crucifix in Cambodia, the one with the leg of Jesus missing, reminded me that we never know when or how we will encounter God. Gaga was a servant.

She could have railed against her fate and lived a life of bitterness and envy. Instead, she embraced it, imbuing her life with a dignity and devotion that shone on everyone around her. The makers of that cross had lost limbs to land mines, deadly contraptions designed with the sole purpose of maiming and disabling. Instead of giving in to the misery that must have brought, these people joined their suffering to Christ, claiming and proclaiming a God who was bearing his pain, bearing the cross.

CHAPTER FIVE

The Maryknoll Sisters

Gaga was not my only unexpected encounter with God in my childhood. Another came because I failed an entrance exam. My father was not a practicing Catholic, but he made sure that we were baptized and that we were enrolled in Catholic schools. When I took the first-grade entrance exam for St. Paul's school, I froze and could not write. I did not get in. But I was successfully placed into the Maryknoll Sisters' School. As my good friend at Notre Dame, Fr. Paul Doyle, C.S.C., told me, "When God doesn't give you what you want, he gives you something better." This is certainly the case with my enrollment at Maryknoll, the place that I spent most of my waking hours over the next twelve years.

The Maryknoll Sisters of the Dominicans was founded in 1912 by a dynamic, adventurous, big-hearted, and faith-filled Smith College graduate named Mollie Rogers. As Mother Mary Joseph, she formed the first American community of religious women whose ministry was focused outside of the United States. From the beautiful motherhouse in Ossining, New York, the Maryknoll Sisters have sent forth into mission over four thousand professed women to Asia, Africa, and Latin America. Their call was not only to serve the poor, but also to live with them and embrace their culture and language while bearing a joy that evoked the love of God for all. China was a main location for their ministry, but by the 1950s, the People's Republic of China had deported them. Luckily for me, they came to Hong Kong and greatly expanded their ministries to include schools, hospitals, clinics, peace and justice programs, and social services for the elderly and disabled.

I received a first-rate education from the sisters. Starting in second grade, instruction in almost all subjects was conducted in English. This was due to necessity: the sisters did not master Cantonese well enough to teach beyond first grade. For us "Maryknoll girls" (a term all graduates are affectionately called, regardless of our current age), it became a point of distinction and pride. Such immersion gave us a command of English that was well known in the colony and made our school very much the "it" school of the day.

My Maryknoll education opened up a view to a world of possibilities and alternative paths that were not generally available to young Chinese women. I could imagine myself being independent like Ah Gaga, but not as a servant. I recoiled at the thought of relying on a husband for an allowance. I had thoughts, ideas, the facility to give expression to these, and the confidence to think that they deserved a chance.

In contrast to the Chinese learn-by-rote approach to education, we were encouraged to think with logic and reason. Since this practice was cultivated in us by the sisters, these approaches to learning and analysis were linked with religion in my mind. Faith and reason: I never knew of the tension between the two until my studies at Notre Dame revealed the history of the struggle to reconcile faith and reason. We were not allowed to rest on our laurels. When we logged easy victories in debates against our peer schools, the sisters arranged for us to compete against native English speakers, the children of British expatriates.

But what we gained from the sisters was so much more than academics, imagination, aspirations, and attitude. We learned about friendship, community, and compassion. This was critical to our formation because in those days Hong Kong operated on a highly competitive elimination system of education, modeled after the British system. Those first-grade entry exams were only the beginning. After sixth grade, there were public examinations in mathematics, English, and Chinese. One out of four students would proceed to the high school of their choice; the others would have to settle for less prestigious schools.

After grade eleven, a student would "sit" for exams in seven to ten subjects, each covering five years of content. I always thought that the British term for taking an exam — "sit" — was a most laughable verb for the experience unless it meant to "sit on nails" or "sit on coals." After these exams, about 20 percent would proceed to the last two years of high school where they would earn the opportunity to be tested again for a small number of places in two major universities in Hong Kong at that time. The pressures were exacerbated by the publication of each student's results in the newspaper!

While that system operated on extreme competition cast in a zero-sum framework — if someone else won, you lost — the sisters developed an esprit de corps among their "girls." We were expected to help each other, to look beyond grades and rankings, to recognize our diverse gifts, and to lift up each other. As we grew together through the years and recognized that our paths would eventually diverge, this helped us treasure each other. The academic pressures from the Hong Kong system were intense, but we did not turn on each other. Excellence to us was not a competitive sport.

In my school, the sisters were educating young women from relatively well-to-do families, but they also ran ministries for the poor and those who lived on the margin. They made home visits to families, squatters who lived in the huts on the hillside of Hong Kong. When government programs provided low-cost housing for these families, the sisters followed to those locales and established hospitals and clinics for the poor, the elderly, and the deaf. They attended to the waves of immigrants who came from China, Vietnam, and Cambodia. Through the Legion of Mary and YCS (Young Christian Students), the sisters shared this work with the Maryknoll girls.

My assignments included duties at the mobile clinics that served the boat people in the Aberdeen area of Hong Kong. These are fisher people who lived on sampans — junks. They had no bathrooms, and little access to health care. On Saturdays, many would come to the mobile clinics for anything from cuts to fevers.

I must admit I was not comfortable holding the arms or feet of the boat people to clean their wounds. The smells, grime, drool, and bio-matter assaulted my senses and made me want to pull back in squeamishness. I was no good at it and still am not. But watching the sisters ministering to them let me recognize what true humility and service to God was about. God calls us to break through these barriers so as to see Him in and beyond the degradation that people live with.

Eventually, my assignments became more cerebral — I gave English lessons after school to young female factory workers who were coming off their day shift in the garment district. I taught them vocabulary, and we practiced basic conversations in English. My father was against my traveling to this neighborhood, often described by a Chinese

word that means "mixed," "complicated," "unsavory." But I
was never in danger.

I liked my students and felt their deep desire to learn
so that they could move out of their sewing sweatshops or
the factories where they assembled plastic everything. For
many, the English language would help them land better-
paying jobs as waitresses in good hotels and, for some,
probably as hostesses in nightclubs. I focused on my lessons, but I did not know how to show that I cared beyond
the difference in the pronunciation of "r" versus "l." In a
way, there was safety in the distance between their world
and mine, between them and me. There was also a guilt that
came with knowing that they were not dealt the same cards
that I was. I always wished that I was more able, less fearful,
so that I could truly engage.

I also taught English to our family chauffeur, Mr. Lai,
a learned Chinese scholar whom I knew well from all the
rides with my father. When I was in sixth grade, we made a
pact that I would tutor him in English while he helped me
with Chinese vocabulary. We both had to face big exams:
his was the certification for a taxi driver's license, which required English proficiency, and mine was the much-dread-
ed sixth-grade public exam. We flourished from each other's
tutoring. Mr. Lai reinvented himself as a proud taxi driver
and would eventually earn a taxi license and purchase his
own vehicle. These are highly valuable assets. They enabled
him to support his family and save for his retirement. It is
an illustration I often used to show how capitalism can be
made to work for those with limited assets. As for me, with
Mr. Lai's help, I moved on successfully beyond sixth grade.

Something else happened during those twelve years
with the Maryknoll Sisters — my faith developed. In the
early years, the nuns in their habits were largely objects

of fascination. Do they wear pajamas? swimming suits? What is their hair like underneath the wimples? How do they move around in those habits in the sweltering heat? Learning about God and the Scriptures was just another subject to be mastered. Going to confession and Mass was ultraspecial because the Catholics were excused from class, and that felt important. On Sunday, when we were driven to Mass by my father, who insisted on our going but never himself came into church, I was more attentive to the display of holy cards and which of my friends were present than the liturgy or homilies.

It was in junior high that I started to ask questions. Why did the sisters leave home and everything they knew to come and teach us Chinese girls whom they had never met? How do they flourish living without their families? Where do they find strength to face the challenges: master new languages, live with poverty, cope with diseases? What is the source of their joy, the spirit of possibility that overflows from them? How do they find the courage to stand up for what they believe and speak truth to power? I eventually concluded that there was only one answer: God must be *very* real for them. Otherwise none of this made sense.

I came to believe that God makes promises and keeps them, and these promises are about love for us. I read it in the Scriptures, and I saw its power in the sisters. This is the foundational belief that emerged from those high-school years at Maryknoll. During every challenge I have faced, every fork in the road, every disappointment, I have held on to this. Every quandary always points to the same question: whom would I bet on to keep a promise — God or something or someone else? The answer has always been simple.

In our last two years at Maryknoll, my friends (Catholic and non-Catholic) and I would make it a practice to visit chapel during our lunch hour. Prayer became relevant because God was listening.

CHAPTER SIX

Letting Go:
From Hong Kong to America

Someone asked me once whether I grew up rich. If "rich" means amenities such as servants, chauffeurs, wonderful dinners, good schools, piano lessons, a thousand-square-foot condo for twelve people in a good neighborhood, then I grew up rich. If "rich" means free of worry, the answer would be *no*.

My father was a brilliant man who excelled in the analytics and business of shipping. But he did not suffer fools and often expressed his opinion in the most unvarnished manner. He was fine as long as people worked hard and spoke clearly about what they did or didn't know or what they did or didn't do. He would not hesitate to point out gaps in logic regardless of the position of the person — whether he was a boss, a peer, or a subordinate. My mother often told the story of how my father stood up to a Japanese soldier brandishing a bayonet when they disagreed. Such mannerisms, probably developed during his years of education in Europe, did not work well for communicating in the Chinese business world where maintaining face with "coded" speech was the norm.

Peter Woo flourished as long as he worked for a British company. But when that British company left Hong Kong in the 1960s — my father turned down a position with them in Vietnam — his employment with Chinese firms was laden with conflict and tension. Even as a young teen, I was aware that my father's job situation and therefore our financial security were precarious.

Making matters worse, my father never developed the practice of saving, leading to a lack of security further accentuated by two other problems: bad health and gambling. My father had part of his liver removed even before I was born; I was not sure whether this was due to alcohol. It may well have been — he seldom drank afterward. But years of smoking and high-cholesterol diets led to a succession of problems, beginning with a heart attack, followed by diabetes, hypertension, and gout.

When the first heart attack happened in 1968, treatment (at least as available in Hong Kong) consisted mostly of bed rest. We were told not to cause stress for my father. I remember going home after my daily hospital visit with a sense of vulnerability that our lives would completely unravel. When I told my nanny of my sense of helplessness, she would tell me to study hard so that one day I could work and take care of my parents, as a responsible Chinese daughter would. She reminded me that she took care of her family by being a servant.

My father recovered, returned home, and went back to work, but did not recover his health totally: his condition was just different degrees of "marginal." Worry was always present.

On top of everything was my father's substantial gambling habit, betting on Mahjong, a game for four people played with tiles. The goal of the game is to assemble a certain pattern of tiles and prevent your opponents from making their hand. It is a game of brainpower and memory. Played for small or big bets, Mahjong is an extremely popular game for all in Hong Kong: it provides both recreation and social exchange.

It is only recently that I could admit to myself that my father's love for Mahjong was an addiction. He played it every night, usually coming home at three or four o'clock in the morning. He played for big stakes with huge winnings or losses. Repeatedly, our condominium was mortgaged. This went on for years. It was hard on my mother, and the tension would erupt into harsh words. Overall, she felt helpless and trapped in a situation she could not make better.

This was our family norm — far from what was considered normal and definitely not sustainable. Eventually, my father stopped playing Mahjong when there were no more funds because the condo could not support any more debt and his income had stopped.

Despite my father's imperfections, he and I were very close. My father adored and admired me. I had the achievements he respected (good grades, awards) without the flaws that he recognized in himself. He could not stop bragging about me to his friends. He would beam when neighbors thanked him for the tutoring sessions I gave their kids. When my father lost his patience and let his temper fly, my nanny and I were the two who could signal disapproval, bringing about some restraint. While pleased that I was flourishing in Catholic education, my father cautioned that I must not take "turning the other cheek" too literally. We had many good times together: boisterous large family dinners where we would compete on who could get the thinnest continuous peel from an orange; restaurant outings for our favorite dishes; and sojourns to the theater for war and kung fu movies.

Amidst the routine and rhythm of our family, we had our share of laughter, celebrations, and worries. Every day

had its joy; every night worries for my parents would return. My affection for my father helped me understand one
lesson about love: you love someone not because he or she
is perfect, but because they are in your life. It was around
this time that I started my daily visits to the chapel at school.

So yes, I grew up rich in many ways, but poor in others. It is no accident that for my doctoral studies, I would
choose the field of strategic management, which addresses
long-term survival and vitality of organizations: the opposite of living from day to day without a sense of security.

To Honor the Family Name

In 1969, as a tenth grader, the issue of college came into
view. It was clear that my two brothers, Paul and Bill, would
be trained overseas as doctor and lawyer to fulfill my father's wishes. The pragmatic Chinese confer worthiness of
academic pursuit primarily on three professions for their
children (actually, their sons): medicine, engineering, and
law. Such expectations for my brothers were fully anticipat-
ed and accepted. Plans for the daughters? None. My sister
Helen finished high school, while Irene and Maureen moved
on to different paths after ninth grade. Both married when
they were around twenty-one. That was the idea of a good
future for daughters — marry well. On that front, prospects
would be dim for me, given that I was the plain daughter.
Even though I was given my mother's Chinese name meaning "delicate," her nickname for me was "Amazon lady." I
was told that my need for logic and my outspoken nature
would not be pleasing to any future mother-in-law.

In my mind, I knew I would need to care for my parents and nanny. I decided that it would be through professional studies and that it would be in the United States. The

latter was probably formed from my years with the Mary-knoll Sisters and exposure to American ways through television and books. It was also a time when civil rights and the peace protests showcased the idealism of Americans: I was hooked. There was also a measure of uncertainty about "sitting" for the qualifying examinations for Hong Kong University. What if I didn't make it? It had become much harder to focus on these exams because my heart was already set on studies in America. My older brother Paul was studying in Canada, and Bill would be joining him. I wanted my chance to study abroad also.

Unfortunately, there were no funds for that. My father had already declared that I would stay in Hong Kong. Additionally, a year earlier he had visited San Francisco with my mother, and they were scandalized by hippies in different stages of undress. My father could not imagine how that would be a proper place for a young Chinese girl. He also wanted to keep the company of a daughter, as four of my sisters and brothers were moving on to other countries.

Without any idea of how I could pull this off, I proceeded anyway, starting with a visit to the United States Information Service, or USIS, which was funded by the United States government to educate people overseas about American culture. The Hong Kong facility had a comfortable reading room stocked with all sorts of publications. I began researching American universities but was honestly lost without any framework, even a basic understanding of exactly what a university was. It was bewildering. I took my practice SAT test there and bombed on my verbal. It was December 31, 1969, the last day before a new decade. Walking down Ice House Street, I wondered what the next ten years would hold for me. I felt the weight of the world: How would I support my parents? my nanny? Would I get a chance to continue my education? There were no answers, just a huge gap between where I was and where I would like to be.

Eventually, both questions resolved themselves. Following my nanny's instruction I studied the dictionary, crammed in some pretty arcane words and expressions (like "salad days"), and did well enough on the SAT. The choice of college was settled when I met an economics professor at Trans World Airlines, where my sister Helen worked. He was on leave from Purdue University, and he told me it was a comprehensive university, and that meant anyone who went there could study anything she wanted! The fact that I had no idea where West Lafayette, or even Indiana, was, or whether Purdue was even a good school, did not matter. Knowing one person from there made it real. I applied and was accepted. I would never run into that professor again. For the next forty years, my home would be in Indiana, all because of a Saturday encounter when I helped my sister collate and staple documents at work.

The real challenges now began: funding and my father. Purdue tuition for foreign students in 1972 was $800 per semester, and room and board was $1,000 for the same time period. I had to raise a minimum of $3,600. My older sisters were working then, and Irene was married. Together, they gave me part of my tuition. While my father never saved, my nanny had started a habit of wrangling $20 of Hong King money (about $2.50 in U.S. money) every Sunday from my father as savings for the three younger children. When she had accumulated a certain amount, she would give the cash to my mother to convert into gold nuggets about the size of a small piece of chocolate. By the time I was eighteen, Gaga had accumulated several thousand U.S. dollars' worth of gold. That also contributed to my college fund. My brother Paul was now a young doctor. He stepped up to help with room and board. My mother, through the ladies' savings circle that she and my aunt started, purchased my suitcases and heavy winter clothing and blankets for the Midwest winters that sounded absolutely forbidding to them. I finally had enough funding for my first year of study!

When it was time, I went to my father and broke the news. He was both sad and proud. My mother might have prepared him for this disclosure. I told him that I had worked hard; that I had resolved the financial barrier; that, like my brothers, I deserved a chance in education; and that, like him, I would flourish in a Western context. He was truly distressed to have me leave, as all of the six children would be gone when he needed our assistance, company, and strength.

I had the first adult conversation with my father when I asked him to treat me as a Chinese son, give me my freedom, and in turn I would support my parents as my brothers were expected to. I would honor the family name of Woo. Besides, my funding was only for one year, so I might not be gone for long. I not only got his approval, but he also bought me a one-way ticket to the United States and allowed me to send his income tax filing to Purdue as part of the information required for foreign students. But it still broke his heart.

Getting Launched at Purdue University

As I contemplated the possibility of leaving Notre Dame for CRS, I remembered how hard it was to leave my home in Hong Kong. Certainly I had fought to do it, but emotionally it was difficult. My nanny had given me from her own small savings a fairly heavy 24-carat gold chain bracelet, my safety net to be used if I needed to buy passage home. She did not want me to be stranded. My mother gave me the advice that no job was beneath me if it was honorable: if the situation required me to pick up a broom, just do so. That was a surprise coming from my mother, who sometimes felt diminished with the loss of the affluent hierarchy in which she grew up. My sister Irene told me to call her in the Philippines any time I needed, not to worry about the charges. I took her up on that offer.

My sister Helen was supposed to use her TWA standby status to travel to the United States with me, stopping first at Disneyland. But no seats were available. So I took off on my own, went through Disneyland by myself, and did not think that it was a small, small world when I was so far from home. I cried through all my rides. I made a promise to myself that the next time I returned to Disneyland, I would be with family, and we would laugh and squeal like the others.

Arriving in Chicago's huge O'Hare airport with two heavy suitcases, back when they didn't have rollers on them, I clutched my chest X-ray to show immigration officers that I was free of tuberculosis. I had to transfer to a satellite terminal for commuter airline Air Wisconsin. That was confusing, and I didn't know where it was located.

Finally arriving at Purdue, I checked into the cavernous, unoccupied Meredith Hall one week before other students. The hallways were deserted, and a toilet flushing sounded like an explosion. The food came in names I had never heard before: chicken tetrazzini (which I liked) and hominy (which I didn't). Even when the other girls started to arrive, I felt like an alien in knee socks and pleated skirts among trendy coeds who wore blue jeans. Many knew each other from high school, campus clubs, band, or whatever. I think freshman insecurity required each to clutch on to a "friend" early on. I found mine, too, in my outgoing roommate Missy and the solicitous counselor Cathy.

On my first foray to register for class, my nonexisting map-reading skills landed me in the Band Office. Feeling utterly incompetent and very alone, I started crying, which led the perceptive receptionist to ask about my religion. "Roman Catholic," I said. She immediately called the local Newman Center — the St. Thomas Aquinas Center — to reach out to me. From that day on, St. Tom's was my home.

When I finally got my schedule, among my fifteen credit hours was "Remedial English," an automatic enrollment for all foreign students. As I only had enough funds for one year of college, I did not want Remedial English and the limit of fifteen credits. Though completely intimidated, I asked, "May I please see a professor?"

I was sent to the kindly Professor Glenn Griffin of the English Department. He had grizzled white hair, sparkling blue eyes, apple cheeks, a warm smile, and a pipe in his mouth. He was close enough to Peter O'Toole in *Goodbye Mr. Chips* for me. I explained that I did not belong in Remedial English, that I had read Shakespeare, Milton, and had debated in English. I also explained that I would like to take as many courses as possible because the Purdue economics professor I met in Hong Kong said I could take anything I wanted. Professor Griffin filled out a form that made Remedial English disappear, put me in his junior-level writing course, and worked with me on my schedule. We started with twenty-four credit hours for the semester, which would eventually drop to twenty-one when I found out what I could handle.

Professor Griffin became my academic counselor, coconspirator in getting permission for this and that, and personal friend. That very night, he and his wife took me to the Purdue Horticulture Park, which was breathtaking in its beauty. Every year, for my birthday, Glenn and Florence would invite my friends and me to their home for cake and cookies.

Kind people populated my life that first year. In addition to the Griffins, Missy, and Cathy, I met Liz, whose parents adopted me and included me in dinners prior to our academic convocations. St. Tom's was a vibrant Catholic student center with faith-filled and gifted leaders in Fr. Leo Piguet, Fr. Leo Haigerty, Fr. Phil Bowers, and Mary Pat Siczek. I went to 11:30 a.m. or 4:30 p.m. Mass daily and spent much time in the common space downstairs or at the center's kitchen. I was the "taster" for the treats that parishioners brought in for the priests. I enrolled for credit in the theology courses offered through the University of Notre Dame, not knowing, of course, that it would become a part of my future.

At night I would stop by St. Tom's on my way from the library to the dorm and entrust to God my worries and recount what I learned that day. The priests and Mary Pat made sure I was covered for the holidays, bringing me home to their families. They attended the academic functions as my family. I did all my extracurricular work at the center and met my husband David when we were elected to the parish council in 1973: he as president and I as secretary. St. Tom's rang the church bells when I successfully defended my Ph.D. dissertation six years later.

In September of my first semester, my father came to West Lafayette after my sister Maureen's wedding in Britain. I could not go to the wedding, as I was in school and could not afford the fare. After breakfast on campus, he wanted to walk with me to my calculus class in the Physics Building. But the trek was longer than his health could handle. He stopped part way and sat on a bench. After twenty steps or so, I looked back and saw him crying. It was a moment I'll never forget. I started a scrapbook for him in which I posted my academic honors. Whenever there was a new recognition, I would send it home for him to add to the collection.

That first year toughened me. The dorm was one mile from my classrooms, and I was walking four to six miles a day. I lost weight. I had little spending money to speak of and used almost all of it to buy aerograms — that now outdated lightweight blue sheet of paper at reduced postage for international correspondence. I found out how I could get by with almost no money: I did not eat out, took advantage of the free social activities in the dorm and church, walked everywhere. I had my hair cut by trainees in the local beauty academy. When my mother sent a box of treats each semester, I paced myself to make them last until the next one came. Because the opportunity would likely end for me after a year, I approached learning as a privilege, and that gave me incredible energy and discipline. There were some hard times, too, including a scolding from a classmate I tutored in calculus who told me that I was not welcome in his country for blowing the curve in the class. But these paled in comparison to the riches I received.

I signed up for classes for the second year even though I had run out of funds for tuition. Even today financial aid of any sort for international undergraduates is rare. But Purdue had an even greater rarity — two full scholarships for international undergraduates. I applied, though I knew the odds were slim. After all, I had one B on my transcript. On the day in April 1973 when the decision was to be announced, I had to make a choice when I got out of my class at 11:20 a.m.: head straight for the International Students Office to get what would certainly be a disappointing result, or go to 11:30 Mass.

Attending Mass would require me to wait for an hour afterward as the International Students Office would be closed from noon until 1:00. But it also allowed me to postpone the disappointment for another ninety minutes and have a good talk with God. In that hour, I gave full force to my frustration and lashed out at God: Why was I born a girl? Why did it have to be so much harder for a girl? How would I take care of my parents and nanny? What more did He want me to do? At Purdue, there were some Hong Kong students who came from well-to-do families: why them and not me? And, when everything fell apart, could He please pick me up and show another way as I had no more ideas?

After Mass, with a heavy heart anticipating the end of my dream, I went to get the letter. A *yes*! I was beside myself with disbelief and relief: three years of full tuition support! I would be able to complete my studies! I could see a path that would give me a future. My brother Paul offered to help me with room and board for the next two years, because I could complete my studies within that time if I carried the same load. This scholarship was the game-changer for me: it was the launching pad that eventually propelled me into graduate education and my career as an academic and academic administrator. It was like tapping into a rich and endless stream of opportunities. It was the difference between looking in from the outside and being on the inside.

Around the time of my undergraduate commencement, my father had a reasonably good stretch both financially and healthwise. He brought my sisters and mother to attend the ceremony. He could not stop beaming, and he met David, who was a good friend at that time and helped me get my family around Purdue. Father observed that David would make a good husband (this was before we started dating) because he did a good job with the maintenance of his car and was working toward a doctorate in Industrial Engineering. It was the happiest gathering of our family ever, and the clouds of worry did not loom over us.

When gambling debts, business ruptures, and bad health finally caught up with him, my father found great joy and solace in the lives and accomplishments of his children. After his passing, among his neatly organized documents, I found the scrapbook I made for him and the graduation program with the page turned down that had my name marked by "one sword and two stars" (his terms for the honors program and academic standing) next to it. When I speak at commencement ceremonies, I share with the graduates that one day they might find their programs in the treasured collections of their parents, grandparents, or other loved ones as I did mine.

In 1979, I completed my doctorate, sent my dissertation to committee members, and got married to David Bartkus on the next day. Our seven years of friendship had blossomed into a romance, and we have been married now for over thirty-five years. I first got a sense of David's kindness and how much he cared for me when he started delivering a donut to my door around four or five o'clock each morning. This was after he finished his computer work at the math building during the graveyard hours allocated for graduate students. I was enrolled in a one-year Master's program that packed in fifty-three graduate credit hours in eleven months. It felt like I never quite went to bed. After I brushed my teeth and changed into pajamas, I would return to my desk, eventually fall asleep there, and wake up with a sore neck and numb arms. David would call in the middle of the night to send me to bed so that I could get some proper rest.

My father lived to know of the completion of my Ph.D. and my marriage to David, but he could not attend the "hooding" ceremony (when a Ph.D. candidate receives an academic hood to signify the new status) or my wedding due to poor health and failed fortunes. For my wedding, I decided to walk down the aisle by myself because I did not want anyone to replace my father. I took out my first loan for the wedding expenses. Changing my last name was not an option because I had made a promise to my father that I would carry on and honor the Woo family name like a son.

From 1972 to 1997, except for two years, I went through my late teens, twenties, thirties, and early forties at Purdue University. I earned three degrees there, became a faculty member, an administrator, and a member of the university leadership team. In 1997, when Notre Dame reached out to me, my professional and family lives were perfect. My research and teaching in strategic management benefitted from the generous and spot-on guidance from former committee members and now colleagues, Professors Arnie Cooper and Dan Schendel. Dr. Ringel (Executive Vice President) and Dr. Beering (President) gave me the most interesting assignments related to university planning as well as developing the culture and capacity for continuous improvement. Dr. Ringel brought me along to his Big Ten provosts' meetings as a way for me to observe how decisions were made. He wanted me to have the experiences and opportunities to someday become a provost at a major university.

When I let Dr. Ringel know that I had accepted a position at Notre Dame, he was pained and could only ask, "Why are you letting a good thing go?"

CHAPTER SEVEN

From Notre Dame to CRS

When Dr. Nathan Hatch became the provost of Notre Dame on July 1, 1996, one of his priorities was to hire a dean for the College of Business Administration. Within that first week of July, he was at Purdue University having breakfast with me when I had made it very clear that I had *absolutely* no intention of leaving. Despite the following courtship, which included sharing with me the college budget, an invitation to a Notre Dame football game, and phone calls from ND alumni, I was unmoved. And our two sons (third and sixth grades) were vehemently opposed to leaving Purdue University.

Two Masses changed everything. Before leaving the Notre Dame campus after the football game, we went to Mass, and the reading of the day recounted the parable of the three servants with their allocated talents (Matthew 25:14–30). The one who buried his got a scolding: "lazy lout," as I recall. I wondered whether it might be me. Then back at Purdue on a beautiful fall day, I walked out of daily Mass and had this sense that I should go to Notre Dame. I could not remember what I heard, but I can still feel that unshakable sense that I had just received my marching orders.

I went home to David with the pronouncement that I think God wanted us to go to Notre Dame. He immediately pledged support and said that we would make it work. I called Nathan to tell him that I would take the position and asked that the process be completed quickly. I knew that if I had gone back to my Purdue colleagues with a possibility, rather than a done deal, I would not be strong enough to reject their plea to stay. I love them as family and did not want to put people through the emotional investments that come with tugs and counteroffers. Besides, I was not looking for something that Purdue could give me. When Tim McGinley, the Chair of the Purdue board, asked for a reconsideration, I told him that I felt "called by the Holy Spirit." As a devout Catholic, he conceded that Purdue would not be able to counter that offer.

At Notre Dame, I was able to put front and center a deep conviction that all business schools, and particularly Notre Dame, must integrate ethical formation with the acquisition of knowledge and managerial skills. In the early days, prior to the Enron scandal, faculty, students, and parents would ask whether recruiters would place a high value on ethics formation since no position descriptions explicitly call for this. Would our students be perceived as quaint? good-hearted but not savvy? unable to make tough business decisions? Peer schools made light of ethics. Would this emphasis lead a school to a top ranking?

Because of my twelve years of education with the Maryknoll Sisters, the idea of such a trade-off was ridiculous to me. I could not imagine a greater disaster than brains and power without values. The foundation for ethical and virtuous behavior for me is our faith.

The notion that success in business precludes ethical behavior also creates another bias: that business is an unworthy pursuit for people of faith and compassion. This bias casts business, at best, as a necessary evil. Having grown up in Hong Kong amidst the large influx of refugees from the People's Republic of China, I saw how essential business was to the advancement of people and society. These accusations dismissed the economic, social, and governance progress that can come from good business practices, particularly for the less fortunate, who stand to gain the most from ethical business behavior.

The Church's teachings through the encyclicals *Centesimus Annus* by Pope St. John Paul II and *Caritas in Veritate* by Pope Benedict XVI, as well as the apostolic exhortation *Evangelii Gaudium* by Pope Francis, indicate that business can be a force for good to serve the poor rather than rule the poor. As Pope Benedict taught, business itself is not good or evil; it depends on the conduct of those who lead it. It is, in fact, the "moral energies" of leaders that we must cultivate.

I felt a great sense of purpose in leading this mission and in the privilege of planting seeds in the hearts of 2,500 students every year. The college had earned the credibility to take this message to the leaders of business and business education. Notre Dame provided a broad and deep tradition to focus not only on academic rigor but also on the ethical and faith foundation of our students. Over 80 percent of Notre Dame's undergraduates are Catholic, and the college had a responsibility to help them grow into their professional identity as people of faith.

I remember telling Bishop John D'Arcy, the Bishop of Fort Wayne-South Bend (our local ordinary), when he asked me about my goal: "As a business school, we will play with the 'big boys' (the highly ranked prestigious schools) and we will win some of the time, but on our terms as a Catholic business school living out our Catholic values." When the Mendoza College undergraduate business program achieved the number one position, it was also recognized as the top school in business ethics. We were able to take our voice and message to a much broader audience, including the accreditation body for business schools and the United Nations. Big corporations could not have enough of our students.

My life of faith also grew at Notre Dame, particularly because of the blessing of integrating God's presence into my daily work. On my first visit with Fr. Hesburgh at Notre Dame, he imparted two pieces of advice. One was to beckon the Holy Spirit as often as possible. "Come, Holy Spirit" has become my mantra in all difficult situations, and the Holy Spirit never disappoints. I almost got to the point of reserving a seat for the Holy Spirit to remind me of the Spirit's presence among us.

Fr. Hesburgh's second statement was to remember that our work is to honor the Blessed Mother — the university is named for her, and mediocrity is not the way we serve her. At Notre Dame, I signed my correspondence "Yours in Notre Dame" to declare our mission and fidelity. It was her inspiration that was, I think, behind the success we had at Notre Dame, and therefore the business school's rise to the top rank was not about bragging rights. It was a testimony that our best work comes from using our talents to fulfill God's call to serve others with justice.

Most mornings at Notre Dame, I would stop at the grotto and "remind" the Father, Son, Holy Spirit, and Blessed Mother that it was a working day and that we all needed to show up. My lifeline was a stop at the Rosary chapel next to the elevators in the Mendoza College, wrapping my hands around a warm mug of coffee and breathing in the aroma. It felt like a chat at the kitchen table of God's home, sharing the routine of the day and the intimacy and hope that underlie such "small" talk.

There was one day in chapel at the end of the Year of Rosary when I felt terribly guilty for not doing enough. I ended my "chat" by promising the Blessed Mother that I would recite all four sets of mysteries by the end of the day. Well, the day was very hectic: by 5:00 p.m. I had not yet broken away to say the Rosary. My older son, Ryan, was on the line with an invitation to have dinner with him. I jumped at that. Afterward, I was so relaxed and tired that I went to bed early. The next day in chapel, I was overcome with gratitude rather than guilt. The previous day's experience felt like a mother sending me what I needed: a special time with my son and rest after many days of running hard. My pledge to say the Rosary was undertaken as duty made in guilt. That, I realized, was not prayer.

But now that we were well settled and everything was going well, CRS called. In my late fifties, would I be up for a career change? Could I handle being uprooted from my community? I was living out, once again, the question Dr. Ringel had put to me, "Why are you letting a good thing go?"

Coming Through, By the Power of God

When I have stepped up to face challenges in the past, feeling overwhelmed and alone, I have turned to God. Praying and pleading, I felt like God was listening and that He would not just leave me to my own resources. I had enough moments when I could not see my way from here to there, and yet somehow I made it through. God was with me. CRS may have been His invitation for me to take on something that is mine to do, mine to contribute.

I have come to appreciate the challenges and disappointments I faced because they were ways to become a better version of myself. They have shifted me toward the paths that align with who I really am or long to be: mind, heart, and soul. Indeed, when we do not get what we ask for, God leads us to something better. I did not flourish in my first two professional positions in private companies. I didn't find the work interesting or the culture supportive. Both paid well and met my early desire to work in big — and big issue — organizations. But in both of these settings I had a discomfort that felt like a vitamin deficiency: I needed something more to be fully me. It was clear that I missed the academic work and culture. To return, I took a substantial pay cut and moved off the corporate ladder, which in those days felt like an admission of failure.

Shortly after that, I bombed at my interview at a very prestigious school when I had no intelligent answer to the question, "How would you react if a student threw a pie at you to test you out?" That really had happened to a young female faculty member, and the only answer I could muster was "not very well."

There were other challenges, such as David's starting two businesses that eventually had to be terminated. It was around the time of the birth of our younger son. Security, which drove how I looked at everything then, took a plunge. Yet all these disappointments, plus others, were the grist that forced us to grow; communicate our needs, fears, and *dreams*; redefine our values; stand by each other; and put our faith in God and step forward with anticipation and trust.

On the receiving end, I have realized the incredible power of kindness, generosity, friendship, and love. These are all manifestations of God that come through people. God sends people into our lives and vice versa. He certainly sent many into mine, from my nanny to my major professor

Arnie Cooper, who directed my doctoral research, to Dr. Steven Beering, the President of Purdue.

At Notre Dame, the priests and sisters of the Holy Cross welcomed us as family. Fr. Paul Doyle, C.S.C., was a brother to my husband, David, an only child, when he faced the loss of his dad and only remaining parent. Fr. Bill Beauchamp, C.S.C., procured the largest pledge for Notre Dame at that time to give the business school the needed boost in our journey to become best in class. On the other side of this pledge, benefactor Tom Mendoza made the commitment with no strings attached except for us to help students live the Notre Dame values in their professions.

Tom Quinn, Notre Dame alumnus and a member of my advisory board, offered me the first one-million-dollar gift to use in whatever way I saw fit. I called this the "sleep well" money, as it allowed me to stretch and take risks. Bill and Joan Hank and their family underwrote our expansion of the nonprofit administration programs to make graduate education affordable for professionals in the social service sector. Benefactors like Roxanne and Rocco Martino and Mark and Karen Rauenhorst gave generously of their treasures and their friendship. My colleagues at Notre Dame, Roger Huang, Bill Nichols, Ed Trubac, Leo Burke, and Mary Hamann, were true friends whose integrity and commitment would do justice to both the words "true" and "friend." People say that a leader's job can be lonely: serving with them would dispel that feeling for me.

God has sent me such people at each step of my life. I knew He would send them again if and when I got to CRS.

In my husband and two sons, I feel God's deep blessings and see His presence. They are faith-filled, kind, slow to judge, and thoughtful of others. David, who came from a completely different background of stability and calm, stepped up to the various crises of the Woo family. He steadied us through these storms while helping me through hurts and wounds from the past. Ryan is a young doctor who has chosen family medicine as his calling and now pursues advanced study in Geriatrics. Each time he stopped at Subway, he would buy a sandwich for himself and coupons for panhandlers. Justin, a doctoral student in theology at Notre Dame, is driven by a deep love for Scripture and the desire to recover the Holy in secular culture.

I have come to understand that my early life, steeped in worry, emanated first and foremost from love for family and the instinctive desire to care for them. In my time as dean, I had conversations with students who were distressed over the job loss of their parents and the corresponding loss of income and savings. They didn't know what they could do, and the emotions ranged from depression to the desire for escape. I would share my experience that love always finds a way; that if they give their best to what they are doing, take advantage of their opportunities, and not recoil from the people in need, God will do the rest.

At a taekwondo lesson when the boys were in second and fifth grades, the instructor was demonstrating the technique for breaking boards with his hand, elbow, and foot. He held up the board and said, "If your eyes focus on the board, you will not be able to break it, and it will hurt. You must visualize your hand, foot, or elbow going *through* the board, and you will make it." I actually had tears in my eyes because that was so true for all the challenges in life. We have to imagine ourselves successfully coming through, with the power of God, on the other side.

The possibility of serving at CRS resonated with something deep and personal. For I could see my nanny in the children who did not have a childhood or proper schooling and those at the bottom of society; I could see my mother in the women who feel helpless in their situations and want greater stability for themselves and their families; I could see my father in those who just need a little nudging to remember that grace is there for the asking. I could see myself in those who need a bridge from here to there. Because I could see God sending people to me in my life, I could see Him sending us to others. Because I have experienced His love, I know it is meant for everyone. God entrusts us to one another and makes us a part of His miracles. This is my *joy*.

So I listened to what God said. And he said, "Go." After this long process, I accepted the presidency of CRS.

That was the decision that led me some months later to be in Cambodia, confronting the horrors of its genocide. But in the midst of such despair, what did I find? Hope. Hope in the crucifix made by the amputee who claimed Christ for himself and his fellow amputees. Hope in the many people I met who had grown up in fear and deprivation and horror and yet found an education and now worked for the future of their country.

I no longer have night sweats, but of course I still have fears and worries. When I do, I can always put on the 24-karat gold bracelet that my nanny Gaga gave me when I left Hong Kong in case I needed to buy a ticket home. God has seen to it that she is there with me; that so many people are there with me. So wherever I am, I am home.

Part II

God Sends Us to Neighbors

CHAPTER EIGHT

Where Miracles Happen

I was feeling excited on the first day in my new office in the CRS Baltimore headquarters in January 2012, like a pupil at the beginning of a new school year, eager to start but nervous. What a journey it had been since CRS President Ken Hackett knocked on the door of my office at Notre Dame nine years earlier. He had come to tell me that CRS's board was opening up its membership to non-bishops, asking if I would consider becoming one of its first lay members.

To tell the truth, I knew little about CRS at the time. I had heard about it for years at church, during the annual Rice Bowl campaign and when various special collections were taken after disasters. I knew that money was going to CRS to help feed the hungry, and to assist those affected by storms and earthquakes. But I had no idea of CRS's size, its scope, its technical sophistication, or how respected it was in the aid community both for its commitment and expertise. I learned so much during the six years I served on the board. But mainly what I learned — in those six years and in the six months since my appointment as president was announced — was how much more I had to learn.

As I sat there that January morning, gazing out on a downtown Baltimore street, I remembered one of the trips I had taken as a CRS board member a few years earlier. It was to Ethiopia. We were visiting a water project, the opening of a new well in a remote community. Our board chairman, then Archbishop — now Cardinal — Timothy Dolan was on that trip, as was my son Justin Bartkus, among others.

In my mind that morning in Baltimore, I could not help but contrast the village we visited with my new office in the CRS headquarters building. Just across the room from where I was sitting was a small bathroom. If I ever went in there and turned on the faucet and water did not come out, you can be sure that maintenance people would quickly be on the job, figuring out what was wrong. But these Ethiopians had never been able to do that, had never turned on a tap and seen water flow. For their entire lives and those of their parents and grandparents, getting water meant making a six-mile round trip by foot to a river and hauling it back. That's what they had to do in order to drink, to bathe, to cook, to live. The job fell mainly on the women and girls — such a huge hardship that not only bent backs but also interrupted educations, as the girls had to spend their days getting water instead of going to school.

I once had a small taste of what they went through while growing up in Hong Kong. The Cold War was raging, and tensions were always high. Despite that, in a longstanding arrangement, Hong Kong bought most of its water from China. In one case of dispute, China decided to teach us a lesson by cutting off our water supply. Water came from our faucets once every four days and then for only four hours.

My family would turn on the taps during those hours, save that water, and parcel it out carefully. I remember taking showers from buckets. And certainly I remember the relief we felt when the restrictions were lifted after a few months and once again water flowed from the taps at any time of the day or night.

In that Ethiopian village south of Addis Ababa, called Koye Jejaba, it would have been considered a luxury to have had four hours of water every four days coming from the tap. My hardship seemed so great at the time, but it was nothing compared to what these people had assumed was their lot in life.

I will never forget what I saw that day in Ethiopia when the project was officially opened and the water began to flow into a trough for the animals. The cows rushed to it even before the water was visible. They could feel the vapor in the air.

My son captured the scene in a blog post he wrote at the time:

> The celebration that went up from the villagers was joyous: rhythmic clapping of hands by the men and hooting and hollering by the women. As two elderly women watched their livestock drink clean water for perhaps the first time ever, they raised their arms to heaven, thanking God in their own tongue for the precious gift they had received. The elders of the community sang to us a song of blessing, recounting the untold suffering of previous years, expressing gratitude to us....

What I realized then is that CRS is a place where miracles happen, where God uses us, unites us, and works through our minds and through our hands to bring hope, to bring reconciliation, and to bring the Good News of the gospel. This institution of which I am now president is truly one of the most precious jewels of the Catholic Church in America. What a responsibility. But mostly, what a privilege, to be called to do such work, God's work, each and every day.

Who Is My Neighbor?

As I began my new job, CRS was looking forward to the seventieth anniversary of its founding in 1943. It began in a world thrown topsy-turvy by the same war that so affected my parents' lives in Hong Kong and China. That year, a group of Polish refugees showed up on the border between Iran and the Soviet Union. They were people who had been almost lost amidst the deadly geopolitical battles. When Hitler and Stalin signed their nonaggression pact, these Poles had been taken prisoner by the Russians and sent to Siberia. When Hitler went to war against the Soviets, now the Poles were Russia's allies. The men were sent to fight. Their families were allowed to leave. Taking a precarious journey, they made their way to Iran.

The world was filled with those displaced by the war. The fate of these Poles attracted attention in the United States, where the Church started War Relief Services to help them. The story of what that organization did for those refugees — many ended up in Mexico — is a book in itself. But clearly that did not take care of the many needs that came out of World War II. War Relief Services continued its work, helping feed, house, and resettle thousands of people in the coming years, before and after the fighting ended.

And taking care of the needs that came from World War II did not end the need in the world. So, in 1955, War Relief Services became Catholic Relief Services as the Church in the United States sought to carry out its gospel mission around the world.

What is that mission? Where does it come from?

I find the answer to those questions in contemplating the three big mysteries in all of our lives: God, neighbor, and self. We discover and celebrate these mysteries in our daily living and encounters with each other. In the Gospel of Mark, Jesus taught us the two greatest commandments: "You shall love the Lord your God with all your heart, with all your soul, with all your mind, and with all your strength," and, "You shall love your neighbor as yourself" (12:30–31). And, importantly, He said one was much like the other. These commandments link those three mysteries: God, neighbor, self. As they draw a line from the Ten Commandments in the Old Testament to the Beatitudes in the Sermon on the Mount, these teachings encompass the guiding principles for a full life. In them, God combines our worship of Him with our love for our neighbors.

That then raises the question: "Who is our neighbor?" In *Deus Caritas Est*, Pope Benedict XVI offered his definition through three parables. In the story of Lazarus — not the one who was raised from the dead but the one who lay at the door of the rich man's house — whose sores even attracted dogs, we learn about blindness (Luke 16:19–31). The rich man did not mistreat Lazarus. He did not evict him. He simply did not see him, continuing with a life of overflowing bounty without even a nod to the extreme suffering at his door.

How could this be? Did he not want to see? Did he once see and then become desensitized? Did he give himself permission to shut his eyes and thereby close his heart? Did he narrow his sight for reasons of selfishness? of guilt? because he felt overwhelmed? Did closing his eyes make the plight of Lazarus less relevant? less pressing? This parable tells us that we must open our eyes to suffering, open our hearts to the people who suffer, and know that they are neighbors in our midst, in our ZIP codes, in our human family.

In the parable of the Good Samaritan who crossed the street to tend to a man who fell among robbers (Luke

10:25–37), Pope Benedict offered the second definition. The neighbor is anyone we encounter in need of help. It does not matter if they are from our community or not, if there has been long-standing enmity between our tribes, or if we must exert extra effort to tend to the situation.

In his third illustration, the parable of the Last Judgment, Pope Benedict located Jesus in our neighbor. As the Gospel of Matthew states, "Amen, I say to you, whatever you did for one of these least brothers of mine, you did for me" (25:40). This makes it clear: Christ dwells in our neighbors. Their needs and cries, verbal or silent, are the cries of God.

As we make our way from childhood to adulthood, we try to answer basic questions. Who am I? Do I matter? As we confront that mystery, we seem to be led inevitably to making the distinction between *we* and *they*. *We:* those like ourselves, often related to us, who share our values, protect us, offer us a sense of belonging and a sense of worth. *They:* those who are different from us (in skin color, language, economic status, whatever), threaten us, compete with us, diminish our security. It becomes *we* versus *they*. We keep track on a win-loss column. At best, *their* welfare is not our responsibility; too often, *their* gain is *our* loss, and vice versa.

What we need to understand is that when God is found in our neighbor, "*we* versus *they*" becomes "*we* versus *God*."

The Gaze of Others

I thought back to my frequent visits to the Grotto at Notre Dame. I always felt a bond with everyone who came there to pray and light a candle. It was as if we were all from the same family. No matter why we were there — students trying to make it through a tough semester or survive a break-up, people petitioning for the health and recovery of a loved one, or young and old people alike trying to see a clear path forward, perhaps to gain foothold in a job or career, or even those who came to propose marriage or, like me, to seek solace and inspiration at the beginning of another day — we were all there with something to share with and offer to the Blessed Mother. Somehow, I always felt that I knew every one of them.

And now, sitting in my new office far from Notre Dame's grotto, the same feeling for the very poor and vulnerable served by CRS washed over me. Even though I had met — and knew that I would meet — only a tiny percentage of the 100 million people CRS touches, none of them is a stranger. At that moment, I felt that I knew them all intimately, as I know my own joys and sorrows. I know them because we share so much. Who cannot feel the pain of a father unable to feed his children, of a mother who has no milk to offer her baby, of a woman who has lost her spouse to war, or of a desperately ill patient who finds no doctor and no medicine for relief of pain and treatment of disease?

When they find they have not been abandoned; when, through our hands, the hand of God reaches for them, their eyes and faces smile, just as ours would, when they find that solutions are possible, that life will be better, that children can go to school, that families can be clothed and fed, that they now have a home. Because we are all human, we cannot ever be total strangers to each other. We actually feel each other's joy and pain. This is the bond we should never try to blunt or break, as it is what makes us part of the human family. We must not shut our eyes as the rich man did to the sufferings of Lazarus.

In the life of faith, God asks us to lose that distinction of *they*, to understand that everyone is *we*. If we claim God, we have to claim our neighbors because He is in them. If we want to be in God's family, we need to understand that everyone else is in His family as well. There are no membership criteria and no membership dues. God's rain falls on all the same, and His sun shines on all the same (see Matthew 5:45). *They* are as glorious as *we* are. All are made in the image of God. That is why C. S. Lewis proclaimed in *The Weight of Glory,*

> There are no ordinary people. You have never talked to a mere mortal. Nations, cultures, arts, civilization — these are mortal, and their life is to ours as the life of a gnat. But it is immortals whom we joke with, work with, marry, snub, and exploit — immortal horrors or everlasting splendors.... Next to the Blessed Sacrament itself, your neighbor is the holiest object presented to your senses.[1]

I used to have an embarrassingly shallow habit. Dreading the prospect of hours of small talk at university dinners with people I had never met, I would call ahead and ask to be placed with friends. If that didn't work, I would rearrange the place cards to ensure that I was with *my* group. Eventually I realized that not only was I failing in hospitality, I was making a terrible assumption that *those people* are not worthy of my knowing. I was missing important opportunities to engage other glorious beings.

I adopted a new attitude. I decided that everyone I met would be interesting; that she or he would have a story to tell; that each story would be a sparkle of love, blessing, faith, joy, sacrifice, devotion, triumph, or even heartache: all transcendent stuff! And, as a result, they were. I found that if you are truly interested and seek to honor rather than to pry, there are unlimited questions to ask. One unintended outcome was that my guests would tell others what a brilliant person I was. That was not my intention, and I had made no profound statements as I merely asked questions about their lives and their loves. The warm glow that emerged from drawing out the joys and commitments that comprise *their* stories and *their* lives was cast on *me* as well.

I realized that in our daily routines and countless interactions we are on holy ground as we meet and engage each other. Sacredness lies in these encounters on a daily basis. If we impose tight boundaries around *we*, then we ultimately reject God in others. There is joy created by just welcoming and dignifying other people, by looking their way and meeting their gaze, by recognizing their gifts and affirming them, by acknowledging their plight and reaching out to give a hand.

And now, at CRS, I was going to be able to do that with 100 million people. What a blessing.

CHAPTER NINE

God Chooses the Weak

When people first found out that I was leaving my position as a dean at Notre Dame to join CRS, they appeared to be quite positive. "Good for you," they would say. But many would then add, "I could not imagine myself taking on such a job."

They seemed to think that the type of work CRS does is only for "special" people, for those who have a "vocation." They must picture fighting the urge to flee as their senses are assaulted by some extreme environment of the kind that people at CRS must deal with — the devastation after a typhoon, the despair of a refugee camp, the disease in a clinic in a remote village, the want amid extreme poverty in so many places around the world. Maybe it is understandable that not everyone from a prosperous country like the United States would want to travel to places where security and basic amenities cannot be guaranteed. But the call to serve the poor is not directed to "special" people, it is directed to *everyone* who pledges to live the Gospel message.

God's call provides no waivers. To those who believe they do not have much to offer, that they are not really capable of making a difference, I say think of the widow in the Gospel of Mark who, after many wealthy people had made large contributions to the church treasury, put in her two small coins. "Amen, I say to you, this poor widow put in more than all the other contributors to the treasury," Jesus said. "For they have all contributed from their surplus wealth, but she, from her poverty, has contributed all she had, her whole livelihood" (12:43–44).

Jesus makes clear that there are no exceptions to this duty to the poor, not those who have reaped a full harvest, nor those who are unworthy like tax collectors and prostitutes, nor those who are self-righteous. There are simply no exceptions. He said, "As the Father has sent me, so I send you" (John 20:21); this commission is directed to the apostles and meant for all of us.

It is precisely because we are not special — not particularly bold, faith-filled, committed, or strong — that God calls us, that he sends us. In fact, it is *because* of our weaknesses that we are chosen. For those who know their weaknesses open their hearts to God and let the power of God take hold. As Paul writes in his first letter to the Corinthians: "God chose the foolish of the world to shame the wise, and God chose the weak of the world to shame the strong, and God chose the lowly and despised of the world, those who count for nothing, to reduce to nothing those who are something, so that no human being might boast before God" (1:27–29).

When I was faced with deciding whether to stay at Purdue University or leave for Notre Dame, I read *God, Country, Notre Dame*, by Notre Dame's longtime president Fr. Ted Hesburgh. After recounting his journey as a young man to the presidency of the university and to his retirement, he remarked, "God has a sense of humor; he chose the weak...."

In the days after His resurrection, Jesus was totally exasperated and disappointed by His disciples: "But later, as the eleven were at table, he appeared to them and rebuked them for their unbelief and hardness of heart because they had not believed those who saw him after he had been raised" (Mark 16:14). Yet in the verse that immediately follows, He sends the apostles off on their mission, saying to them, "Go into the whole world and proclaim the gospel to every creature" (16:15). Christ was commissioning not the holy apostles we usually put on pedestals, but those in whom he was disappointed.

So it is that we, who so often disappoint Him, take our place in the world. A prayer usually attributed to St. Teresa of Ávila expresses this call to be the "hands," "feet," "eyes," and "body" of Christ.

> Christ has no body but yours,
> No hands, no feet on earth but yours,
> Yours are the eyes with which he looks
> Compassion on this world,
> Yours are the feet with which he walks to do good,
> Yours are the hands, with which he blesses all the
>   world.
> Yours are the hands, yours are the feet,
> Yours are the eyes, you are his body.
> Christ has no body now but yours,
> No hands, no feet on earth but yours,
> Yours are the eyes with which he looks
> compassion on this world.
> Christ has no body now on earth but yours.

In the Gospels Jesus repeatedly issued the invitation, "Come, follow me," "Come and see," or, "Come dine with me." I am sure most of us would say that we have never received such an invitation, that if we had we would certainly have responded. Maybe we haven't received an exquisitely embossed card or a middle-of-the-night wake-up call or a bolt of lightning that struck us blind like Saul on his way to

Damascus. But God does call — every day, actually. In each moment and in every encounter there is an invitation.

During His agony in the Garden of Gethsemane, Jesus beseeched His disciples: "Stay here and keep watch with me." This invitation still stands today with the plaintive plea, silent or spoken, of the many who suffer tremendous agony: the hungry, the sick, those forced to flee to refugee camps where security cannot be taken for granted and the whereabouts of loved ones are unknown. The most searing pleas to us at CRS come from countries torn apart by violence, where mass evictions, burnings, bombings, and death rule the day. The bishops and our local partners say to us, "Please stay, do not abandon us, do not forget us, let the world know about us."

Rarely does the call from Christ come with such piercing urgency. Instead, it is often an invitation to be compassionate to someone even when you feel he doesn't deserve it; to spend time with and for another when you are pressed for time yourself; to take a path that you had not intended. After high school, I felt the call to be responsible for my parents and nanny, to be ready to provide for them eventually, and took a different path from my friends. I felt alone and burdened. What I did not yet know was the growth and joys that were to come because I took that path.

Now I know for sure that any step taken for love will definitely be a walk with God who — as the story and poster of the single pair of footprints in the sand promises — will carry us when we need Him to. When I made my moves from Purdue to Notre Dame and Notre Dame to CRS, I thought I was doing them for God. But God was doing them for me, as I was the one who was showered with blessings of personal growth, professional maturity, friendship, affirmation, and the joy that comes from seeing something you build flourish, from taking steps on the journey of faith.

Answering the Call

Too often, the first thing that comes to mind when we think of a call from God is that it will mean a sacrifice from us. So maybe we hope the knock on our door does not come too often and, when it does come, it's only on our terms, when we are ready. Don't we always have something else more pressing that we need to take care of? The poor don't need our help. They should help themselves. They are the government's responsibility. And what about the really rich people? Ask them.

But the call to serve is actually like a gift that we find under the Christmas tree, the most exquisite pearl, or the greatest treasure. In some ways, it is the source that sustains life itself. Through it we might find our ultimate purpose, making all our efforts at answering that call feel like a privilege.

Fortunately, there are people who understand this. In my first weeks and months at CRS, I came to see that attitude in so many of my new colleagues, people who were drawn to serving the poorest and most vulnerable as their life's calling. And they keep coming. Our International Development Fellows program is for those just starting out in this field. Many have experience elsewhere. All have graduate degrees. They could certainly earn more money in some other field of work. But for our twenty positions there were more than seven hundred applicants.

I would come to see members of our staff work to improve their skills at helping the poor, learning a third or fourth language, getting another graduate degree, taking on a hardship assignment, turning down offers for much bigger salaries in business. You can see the joy, life, passion, and love in their faces, gestures, steps, and cadences. They were — and are — smart enough to recognize and accept the invitation to the really cool party, the one that came from God.

Sometimes we do say, "No." Sometimes we do feel overwhelmed, fatigued, and bombarded with so much need in the world. When we take a timeout, let it not be a "cop-out" but a period of reading and learning, of praying and listening, of gathering the physical and spiritual strength we will need for resuming active duty in service to God and neighbors. Let us hold ourselves accountable, to determine when and to what we would be willing to say, "Yes." And when we say "Yes," we must follow through. We are reminded in the Gospel of Matthew that the son who said "No" to the father when asked to work in the vineyard but changed his mind and went into the field is better than the one who said "Yes" and did nothing (cf. 21:28–31).

Fortunately for us, God's call to love and serve our neighbor is not a one-time event; it happens all the time, repeatedly, unrelentingly. As long as we do not close our eyes, ears, and hearts, we will see the invitations. There are second chances every day as He keeps putting people who need help in our paths, in our news, in our communities, sometimes in our families. He offers us so many ways to contribute to taking care of the poor. No one needs to feel unable. I have encountered so many "ordinary" people doing things that inspire me and fill me with hope — from tithing 10 percent of their income to the Church, to starting their own charities, to volunteering. And over the years I had come to know so many who have transitioned from industry careers to work at Catholic Charities, to manage food banks or run low-cost housing programs, to become deacons, to receive training as pastoral associates, or to enter as late religious vocations.

And now I was meeting so many like them at CRS.

One way of answering the call from God to assist those in need is with prayers and advocacy. When South Sudan was preparing to have a referendum on its independence in 2011, most thought the country was headed for a disaster that would be a replay of its decades of brutal civil war. Realizing the possibility of a return to violence and immense human suffering, the Catholic Church mounted a global campaign that involved education, prayer vigils, fundraising, and outreach to governments. Through Catholics Confront Global Poverty, an Internet platform sponsored by the United States Conference of Catholic Bishops and CRS, individuals in the United States learned about the situation in South Sudan and were invited to lend their voices to advocate for peace. On the ground, CRS, as it continued development work in this very poor country, partnered with the Church in South Sudan to spread the message and reality of peace, through education, through confrontation, and through reconciliation. The result was a peaceful referendum and transition that amazed the world. In other words, a miracle.

CRS is a place where such miracles happen, where ideas become reality, where what ought to be becomes what is, where God's plan is a map that we try to follow wherever it may lead. The commands of the gospel are not abstract here, they are concrete.

When my predecessor Ken Hackett took on this job in 1992, the agency faced a different kind of challenge than the one presented to me. During its five decades up to that point CRS had grown in size and respect as development aid had become an important part of U.S. foreign policy during the Cold War. But in some ways, CRS had begun to resemble any other secular aid agency. Ken was charged with, essentially, putting the "Catholic" back in Catholic Relief Services. He set out to do this with an agency-wide examination and discussion, really a mission of soul-searching, asking almost everyone involved to think about this essential question: What difference did it make that we were Catholic?

Just as this was being undertaken, the horrific genocide in Rwanda erupted in 1994. CRS was active in Rwanda. According to reports filed at the time, everything was going well, tasks were being accomplished, programs were successful. And then eight hundred thousand people died. How did we not see this? How could we say we were doing our job, helping people improve their lives, when we were missing — or ignoring — a problem that resulted in such a loss of life? What good does it do to work with people toward economic development if they are going to be killed, or become killers? The genocide not only set back all the good work we were doing, but in some way made it meaningless. Had we really accomplished anything?

It was a real stare-into-the-abyss time, not just for CRS but for a lot of aid agencies. And it happened just as we were beginning this self-examination of our Catholic roots, further accelerating that process. It made us go deeper into that question of what we as Catholics, as a Catholic agency, had to offer that made us different. Wasn't it our fundamental responsibility to ensure that the people we were serving were not killed, or killers? If we couldn't do that, why were we bothering with the rest of it?

These are tough questions. And this was a very tough time at CRS.

The Lens of Catholic Social Teaching

What emerged from our soul-searching was in no way a turning away from the size and scope and expertise that CRS had developed. But it was a greater commitment to our gospel mission. The Holy Spirit led the agency to the body of work known as Catholic Social Teaching, and it was here that CRS anchored its faith foundation. Catholic Social Teaching dates from the late nineteenth century. It first emerged as a series of principles developed in response to the industrial revolution that was reshaping the social and economic landscape of Europe. That was when the world Charles Dickens described was quite real. The growth of factories led to huge overcrowded cities and exploited workers, including children. Their labor supported a highly privileged upper crust.

Obviously, there had been class structures and economic and social divisions and exploitation in society throughout the history of the Church. But the rather sudden move from an agrarian to an industrial economy introduced stresses and tensions that probably had not been seen since the end of feudalism. This was the situation that Marx addressed in his writings, which were gaining a widespread following as the industrial revolution traversed Europe.

By contrast, Catholic Social Teaching deals with these injustices by emphasizing the dignity and worth of the individual. It opposes the collective solutions that Marxists endorsed, eventually to such tragic ends as those first refugees served by CRS at the Iranian border could attest. Many of them had been forced to work on Stalin's collective farm. Those farms led to famines that caused the deaths of millions.

The founding document of Catholic Social Teaching is Pope Leo XIII's encyclical *Rerum Novarum — On Capital and Labor*, from 1891. In it he wrote, "In protecting the rights of private individuals … special consideration must be given to the weak and the poor."[2]

There is one foundation of CRS's work: the preferential option for the poor.

Rerum Novarum also states: "Workers are not to be treated as slaves; justice demands that the dignity of human personality be respected in them."[3]

The justice lens we use to examine every program we undertake is to make sure that no matter what its specific intent, it advances the cause of justice and does not create injustice. For instance, if we drill a well, we need to ensure it is doing more than quenching thirst, that it is healing divisions, unifying communities, reinforcing dignity — and also make sure that it is not doing the opposite, which a well can if it is in the wrong place, its bounty available to only certain members of a community, excluding others.

As Bl. Pope Paul VI taught, "Development [is] the new name for peace,"[4] and also that "if you want peace, work for justice."[5]

Catholic Social Teaching also introduced CRS to other concepts that shaped how we approach our work, such as integral human development and subsidiarity (see *Caritas in Veritate*). Integral human development tells us that it is not enough to do just one task — say, delivering food or agricultural training — without taking into consideration how that fits in with all the needs of a person and his community; not just food, but also proper nutrition, medical care, education, access to capital, peace among communities, and so on. All must have a way to sit at the Lord's table in its full munificence.

Subsidiarity tells us that we must listen to those closest to the ground, meeting their needs through local initiatives rather than imposing solutions from afar that are not relevant to the actual situation. That is why we always work through local partners — some 1,200 around the world — supporting them and learning from them, as they implement the programs. The Church is our preferred partner — about half of our partners are Church-related — for good reason. Everywhere in the world, its schools and clinics are not just at the end of the road, but down the path that goes off the end of the road. There we find religious congregations and Catholic ministries whose calling is helping the poorest of the poor, never seeking the spotlight, content to serve.

All of our employees, some 5,000 around the world, are instructed on these principles of Catholic Social Teaching, on how essential they are to the work that we all do. They inform our every act.

Even more fundamentally, CRS exists to make real an essential aspect of our faith — action. Right after delivering the Sermon on the Mount and its profound teaching, Jesus must have been facing people listening with rapt attention, their hearts touched with love for God and neighbor and their eyes opened to the vistas of a world beyond what they could imagine. What did he do at that moment? He called for action. "And everyone who listens to these words of mine *but does not act on them will be* like a fool who built his house on sand. The rain fell, the floods came, and the winds blew and buffeted the house. And it collapsed and was completely ruined" (Matthew 7:26–27, emphasis added).

Jesus taught not only with his words, but also with his own actions: he healed the sick, raised the dead, fed the hungry, welcomed children, invited people to dine with him, walked with them, cried with them, reached out to those deemed to be outcasts. He even rescued a new couple and their families from embarrassment when wine ran out at the wedding. There is simply no other way to sustain or grow in our faith without acting on it.

To the proclamations of love from Peter after the resurrection, Jesus responded, "Feed my lambs," "Tend my sheep," "Feed my sheep" (John 21:15–17). When Jesus sent the apostles to spread the Good News, essentially they were to *"do"* the Good News. Faith may stir our sentiments and emotions, but it cannot end there. Listen to what the book of James tells us: "If a brother or sister has nothing to wear and has no food for the day, and one of you says to them, 'Go in peace, keep warm, and eat well,' but you do not give them the necessities of the body, what good is it? So also faith of itself, if it does not have works, is dead" (2:15–17).

In other words, just as the body is dead without food, so faith is dead without action. Thus CRS was established to act on our faith: to reach out, assist, and enhance the lives of the poorest and most vulnerable regardless of their nationality or their creed. For all the downside of modern communications technologies, they do broadcast the plight of people from around the world into our homes. About 20 percent of the world's population lives on $1.25 a day or less; more than 800 million go to bed hungry; ironically, many of these are farmers and their families. Seven million children younger than five years of age die per year — many of them did not have a chance. Fifty percent of women in sub-Saharan Africa deliver their babies without access to clinics or midwives. It is not enough to merely wish these individuals a better future. We must act.

Our faith compels us to bring the love of God to those in need, which Pope Benedict XVI made clear in *Deus Caritas Est* must be rendered without any conditions. We make real God's promise of His presence when we attend to individuals in desperate situations without homes, food, water, livelihood, safety, medical care, or education. We cannot wish these problems away; our part is to put shoulders to the wheel, hands to the plow, and minds to the challenges. In the book *Charity: The Place of the Poor in the Biblical Tradition,* Professor Gary Anderson observed that in early Christian art, almsgiving and the celebration of the Eucharist are depicted together as requisite pathways to God, and that "mitzvah," the Hebrew word for acts of goodness, is also the word for all God's commandments.

From its inception, CRS has performed these acts on the basis of "need, not creed." There was never any *we* and *they*; all are our neighbors. At another water project in Ethiopia, in an arid district in the east known as Dire Dawa, the Catholic Secretariat drilled a new well with a drilling rig donated by CRS. A Muslim woman, who was filling her five-gallon container with water from a tap, was asked what she thought of the installation.

"It's wonderful," she said. "Look how clean this water is. Our life has changed."

When asked who provided such a bounty for her community, she put down her container as a puzzled expression came across her face.

"They call themselves Catholics," she said, "and we give thanks to God for their work."

Does the Good News get any better?

CHAPTER TEN

Lead, Kindly Light

In the first few weeks of my work at CRS, I felt the fears and anxieties, the ones that had made me hesitate to say "Yes" to this wonderful opportunity, melting away. Of course I could find someone new to cut my hair. I could find doctors and dentists and whatever else I needed. I could form new relationships even as I maintained my old ones. How silly it seemed that I had let such concerns distract me now that I contemplated the great work and the importance of the organization I was blessed to lead.

I took an apartment just a few blocks from CRS headquarters. We kept our home in South Bend, and David remained there with his work. I was travelling for CRS so much I was hardly home — either in Baltimore or in South Bend — anyway.

When it was founded, CRS was headquartered in New York. Some of its earliest offices were in the Empire State Building. In 1945, the Army pilot of a B-25 bomber became disoriented over Manhattan and crashed the plane into the seventy-fifth floor of what was then the tallest building in the world. It hit the offices of War Relief Services, killing eleven staff members who were at work on a Saturday. We still remember and honor their service.

The change of name to Catholic Relief Services came in 1955, after many war refugees had been resettled, destroyed houses had been rebuilt, destroyed lives had been put back together.

The move to Baltimore came in 1989. Real estate was cheaper, meaning more money for the poor overseas. And it was a move to a city that looms large in the history of Catholicism in America. A few blocks north and east of CRS headquarters is Baltimore's basilica, the first cathedral built in this new country. Envisioned by the United States' first bishop, John Carroll, and designed by Benjamin Henry Latrobe, architect of the capital in Washington, the basilica was started in 1806 and completed in 1820. Its design turned away from the Gothic structures of the Old World and proclaimed the New in clean geometric lines. Seventeen saints had graced this basilica with their visits.

About fifteen years after the Baltimore move, CRS made another one, into a beautifully renovated building that was once a department store when this part of downtown Baltimore was the city's thriving shopping district. That era came to an end three decades ago, and many buildings in the neighborhood had been abandoned, boarded up, and vandalized. But CRS wanted to be part of the city's rebirth and so committed itself to this building whose renovation includes cutting-edge environmental measures. Over four hundred of CRS's employees work here, their presence an important positive impact on the area.

Despite the progress made in so many parts of Baltimore, my walk to work reaffirmed for me that poverty is not an abstract concept, it is a daily reality, not only for thousands in Baltimore, but for millions around the world. We must keep our eyes open to all of our neighbors, near and far, as we are all part of God's family.

Thinking Strategically

Almost immediately, I took on the task that I felt the board had hired me for — asking everyone at CRS to begin another difficult but necessary journey to find the answer to some basic questions. What is this organization about? What structure should it have as we move into a future fraught with challenges? This was an agency-wide process, engaging everyone to envision and construct a strategy and structure that could carry us far into the twenty-first century.

Our unshakable foundation in this was our faith. We all recognized that CRS would not exist without that. We do the work we do because we believe that God has called us to help the poor. Our foundation in faith motivates us in ways that make CRS stand out among humanitarian agencies.

Faith calls on us to serve the common good with uncommon excellence. As Pope Benedict wrote in *Caritas in Veritate*:

> To desire the *common good* and strive towards it *is a requirement of justice and charity*.... The more we strive to secure a common good corresponding to the real needs of our neighbors, the more effectively we love them. Every Christian is called to practice this charity, in a manner corresponding to his vocation and according to the degree of influence he wields in the *polis* (7).

Polis — that's a word of Greek origin defined by the Merriam-Webster Dictionary as "a state or society especially when characterized by a sense of community." As citizens of the most prosperous and influential country in the world, we have a great deal of influence in the *polis*, in the community of human beings, so our call to practice this charity is particularly strong.

When War Relief Services started, the work it did was of a different nature than what CRS was undertaking seven decades later. Then our job was to get people devastated by war back on their feet so that they could walk as before. But when you move your focus to those who have always been poor, you are dealing with people who have never been on their feet. Some could not be helped to climb the economic ladder because even the bottom rung had been out of their reach.

You can build a school, but what if there are no teachers? Or what if the children cannot attend because they spend their days getting water from a faraway river? You can build a house, but what if there is no food? What if the farms nearby do not produce enough?

There is the familiar proverb: "Give a man a fish, and you feed him for a day. Teach a man to fish, and you feed him for a lifetime." Giving a man a fish is known as resource transfer. It is the most basic and, to many, the most iconic, of charitable act — almsgiving. It is what CRS does after disasters and in emergencies when people have lost the basics. We give them food, we give them water, we give them shelter, as we did for those in need during and after the disaster that was World War II.

The teaching-to-fish part is skills transfer. And CRS is often engaged in that, whether it is instruction in better agricultural techniques, nutrition strategies, approaches to health, or simply reading, writing, and arithmetic.

But what if conflict means that the person you have just taught to fish can't get to the river to put in his line? Or what if his group is not allowed access to the river because of long-standing prejudice? Or what if only boys get to go to the river, not girls? The challenges are many. We use all of the tools that God gave us to confront them.

As Pope Francis has said:

> It is not enough to offer someone a sandwich unless it is accompanied by the possibility of learning how to stand on one's own two feet. Charity that leaves the poor person as he is, is not sufficient. True mercy, the mercy God gives to us and teaches us, demands justice, it demands that the poor find the way to be poor no longer.[6]

Following the tenets of Catholic Social Teaching, CRS takes a holistic and integrated approach to working with a variety of partners — church and secular, private and public. The focus is on the individual, family, and community. Our goal is for each person we encounter to reach his or her full human potential. That means paying attention to the entire person — physical, mental, and spiritual.

We consider our work evangelizing, but not proselytizing. We follow what is written in *Deus Caritas Est*:

> Charity … cannot be used as a means of engaging in what is nowadays considered proselytism…. A Christian knows when it is time to speak of God and when it is better to say nothing and to let love alone speak. He knows that God is love (cf. *1 Jn* 4:8) and that God's presence is felt at the very time when the only thing we do is to love (31c).

In all of our service, we feel a strong sense of accountability to achieve sustainable improvements because we have been entrusted with resources by the United States

Catholic Church and other donors. They have given us their treasures, prayers, affection, and confidence to bring their love in a world of hurt. The poor do not deserve our second best, but our very best. The latter requires us to be self-aware, vigilant, and willing to learn and innovate.

We know that there is no conflict between compassion and excellence; indeed we find that our pursuit of excellence comes directly from our compassion. It is by being compassionate that we come to understand the needs of the poor. They are not just our beneficiaries, they are our teachers. We listen to them, we do not command them. This makes our work so much more effective. Listening, humility, and respect for the people who invite and welcome us into their lives are necessary steps to excellence.

The aid world is strewn with failures that were imposed from the top down. Success, as the concept of subsidiarity teaches us, takes the opposite direction. It is developed on the ground in Burkina Faso or Bangladesh; in Malawi or Mindanao. As Pope Benedict wrote in *Deus Caritas Est*, "This proper way of serving others leads to humility. The one who serves does not consider himself superior to the one served" (35).

Anyone who has ever run a business understands a variant of this very well — serve your customers, and you will find success.

Untying the Knots

By temperament, I am a worrier. All through my childhood, I internalized that role for my family. When I first met my eventual husband, he was a graduate student in industrial engineering. But what most impressed me about David was the fact that when we worked on parish social functions together, he made lists of all the things that could go wrong. By selecting strategic management as my expertise, I became a professional worrier. And that is the role I was undertaking at CRS.

There was much to worry about. The fast-changing funding environment; the increased expectations of our donors for demonstrable, sustainable improvements; the security of our beneficiaries, staff, and partners in conflict zones; well-intentioned but misguided regulations demanded by donors that could diminish our flexibility and sometimes even endanger local partners. And that was only the beginning of my list.

CRS is a complex organization, and achieving coordination between the field and headquarters — as well as among different geographical locales, administrative functions, and various sectors — requires dynamic adaptation and constant attention. Success sometimes requires achieving outcomes that might seem to be in competition with each other.

As we undertook our strategic review, we would need to continue to meet the all-consuming and urgent needs of beneficiaries today while attending to the root causes embedded in unjust structures or conflicts in a society, all the while navigating the balance between stability and innovation, autonomy and standardization, investment and cost controls, honest feedback and authentic support for individuals, accountability and room for mistakes.

Because of our very broad geographic and program portfolio and our representation of the Catholic Church in the United States, our stakeholder groups are almost boundless. These include the Church in the United States, which comprises 195 dioceses of clergy and laypeople who hold a range of opinions about how to implement its social mission; the Vatican; sister Caritas agencies; the Church of the countries in which we work; political, social, and other religious leaders in these regions; different branches and agencies of the United States government — in Washington and in offices around the world — that impact our funding and set the regulatory framework for our operations; foundations and multilateral institutions such as the United Nations and Global Fund; and technical gatekeepers in the sectors of programming we offer. As CRS does not participate in any program or seek funding from any grant that involves artificial family planning, we must also constantly keep abreast of changing specifications by our institutional donors. A former colleague at Notre Dame, after listening to my description, remarked, "Carolyn, you really do not have much control over your environment!"

At times I felt the threat of being overwhelmed by these worries, but then I realized that such challenges are part of many peoples' work. So many of us have our attention hijacked by what we face today when we know we need to be looking to the future. Throw in too little sleep and exercise and relaxation and prayer, not enough attention to simple human contact with family and friends — a choppy phone call from the car as cell signals come and go does not count — and our ability to function is diminished. Even for people who work on behalf of the Church in her various ministries — social services, parish work, health care ministries, and education — who presumably work *for* God have actually driven out quiet time *with* God.

When I first joined Notre Dame, recognizing the need for a different way to approach my work, I sought and found a spiritual advisor in Fr. Paul Doyle, C.S.C. In our first meeting, he had me recite the first two verses of Psalm 127:

Unless the LORD build the house,
>they labor in vain who build.
Unless the LORD guard the city,
>in vain does the guard keep watch.
It is vain for you to rise early
>and put off your rest at night,
To eat bread earned by hard toil —
>all this God gives to his beloved in sleep.

In the years that followed — many years, as I am a very slow learner — I gradually reoriented my thinking as prompted by the first verse and changed my habit as suggested by the second. It is easy to be lost in our work and, with the most admirable sense of responsibility, think that it all depends on us. For the past decade or so, I have realized that my work does not all depend on me, that God is very much a part of our efforts, that the Holy Spirit multiplies our work and sends us the richest harvests.

Working at CRS was leading me to the understanding that, actually, it is not that God has a part in my work, but that I have a part in His work — a liberating sense of who is in charge and who is the helper. Perhaps it is out of necessity at CRS that I learned to surrender to God. I knew I had a tremendous responsibility as I sought realignment of this organization with external factors that were beyond our control using internal levers we could dictate. I now know that the final responsibility for how things will turn out belongs to God.

Beyond the foundational teaching to love Him and to love one another — particularly those among us who have little else — the wisdom and the plan of God are beyond our knowledge. I do not flee from seemingly intractable problems: the tug of disagreements between important stakeholders, the divisive and wrong-headed politicization and polarization of the Church's social and life missions, the darkness of inhuman brutality we see too often in too many places around the world, the oppression of people who are denied the requirements for human dignity. But ultimately I turn these back to God. I recognize that the Church and the world, no matter how imperfect, are ultimately the instruments that God has chosen to carry on His work of unconditional love and to reveal His glory and mercy. Into our self-centered world He came to become one like us, subjected Himself to the acts of our brokenness, and taught us to forgive and love.

While I wish that occasionally someone would part the Red Sea that is in front of me and grant an unimpeded journey along a pathway that is always wise, logical, cohesive, grace-filled, and compassionate, I recognize that the impediments are exactly the way of the Cross; our personal and collective salvation comes not from avoiding these obstacles, but from how we engage them. In the end, our part is a privileged one but small and short in the overall scheme of God's creation. We should give our best but, beyond that, know that this is God's work and we do not have to tie ourselves up in knots when we cannot foresee, forestall, or resolve the issues and challenges. We take one step at a time, seeking God's guidance as Cardinal John Newman so beautifully penned in his poem "The Pillar of the Cloud," set to music as the hymn "Lead Kindly Light":

> Lead, Kindly Light, amid the encircling gloom
>> Lead Thou me on!
> The night is dark, and I am far from home —
>> Lead Thou me on!

Keep Thou my feet: I do not ask to see
The distant scene — one step enough for me.

When I was at Notre Dame, I would start my day in prayer at the Grotto. Now, at CRS, I continue this practice in the beautiful chapel, St. Stephen's, that is part of our headquarters building. As at Notre Dame, before I end my prayer session, I note to the Father, Son, Holy Spirit, and Blessed Mother that this is a workday and that we all need to show up. Before every difficult meeting or event, I repeat Fr. Hesburgh's invocation, "Come, Holy Spirit."

As we join Christ in His work, we have to remember what His invitation offers, not only duty but also succor. "Come to me, all you who labor and are burdened, and I will give you rest," Jesus said. "Take my yoke upon you and learn from me, for I am meek and humble of heart; and you will find rest for yourselves. For my yoke is easy, and my burden light" (Matthew 11:28–30).

That echoes the Old Testament verses found in the book of Jeremiah:

Blessed are those who trust in the LORD;
    the LORD will be their trust.
They are like a tree planted beside the waters
    that stretches out its roots to the stream:
It does not fear heat when it comes,
    its leaves stay green;
In the year of drought it shows no distress,
    but still produces fruit. (17:7–8)

Therefore we can set bold goals. Let go, let God.

CHAPTER ELEVEN

A Bountiful God

During Advent of my first year at CRS, the Gospel reading for Mass one day recounted the story of the paralytic who was lowered from the roof of the house into the place where Jesus was teaching. At the words, "... your sins are forgiven.... I say to you, rise, pick up your stretcher, and go home," the man picked up his mat, walked home and gave glory to God. What caught my eye that Sunday was the last sentence of the passage, which I had hardly noticed before: "Then astonishment seized them all and they glorified God, and, struck with awe, they said, 'We have seen incredible things today'" (Luke 5:20, 24, 26).

As I thought about those words, I was struck by the realization that our work at CRS engages us every day in acts that are "incredible."

How else would you describe a woman facing a death sentence because she carried the human immunodeficiency virus (HIV) who is now flourishing with the health and stamina she needs to care for her children?

Or the mother who was about to sell her daughter but instead learned a trade so she could afford to raise her?

Or a twenty-month-old child weighing nineteen pounds who received treatment to stop and reverse what would have been lifelong damage from stunting?

Or a woman trafficked into the sex trade, who had lost all hope, but in therapy learned how to embroider, rediscovering her sense of beauty and meaning, and through dance found a new way to experience her body with joyful leaps and the ringing of bells that came from her bangled feet?

Or an entire village spared from malaria because generosity from unknown sources made treated bed nets available?

Or a young gang member on the road to a life of violence and retribution who instead took a path of education and training that developed his potential and opened opportunities so that he could be reunited with his family?

That moment of contemplation of the verse in Luke made me realize how much our work at CRS gives us a part in God's miracles. Because we have seen all these things, incredible things, on so many days.

Human hands and divine intervention: an unbeatable partnership! While we still face devastating poverty and suffering, we should also note the significant strides that have been made over the past two to three decades. Consider that in 1990, 12.4 million children younger than five years old died. The figure is now nearly half that, even though the overall number of births has increased. Is that still too many? Yes. Is it progress? Yes. Even as we lament the former, we should celebrate the latter.

In that same time period, again through the collective work of all humanitarian actors, two billion people gained access to clean water sources, and certain diseases such as ringworm were eradicated throughout the world. Another improvement: 76 percent of girls in sub-Saharan Africa have access to some education. And I am sure you have read how many of the world's fastest growing economies are in Africa. Many point to this to say that aid is not the way to help people, that what they need is economic growth. But when I look at those figures, I see the payoff in years of aid work. Hungry people do not make good workers. Sick people do not show up at work. The uneducated do not grow economies. By dealing with such challenges, humanitarian work laid the foundation for Africa's current economic success.

It is never enough. There is always more that can and must be done. This economic growth must benefit all, not just the privileged few. But the daily high from working at CRS is seeing new life, rebirth, recovery, restoration, and renewal: all forms of healing and making whole! Our work is multiplied by God in ways that we cannot even dare imagine. No matter how much or how little we have done, what is finally achieved sparkles with a grace, cohesiveness, and impact that are transcendent and not just from the labor of our own hands. As with the harvests in our fields, we may plant the seeds, irrigate the crops, pluck the weeds, but it is God who sends the sun and the rain, who provides the land.

On this point, in the Maryknoll Sisters' archives I ran across a statement written in 1936 by the founder of the Maryknoll Sisters, Mother Mary Joseph:

> There is nothing more astonishing than life,
>   just as it is,
> nothing more miraculous than growth and change
>   and development, just as revealed to us.
> And as happens so often when we stop to regard
>   God's work,
> there is nothing to do but wonder and thank God,
> realizing how little we planned,
> how little we achieved,
> and yet how much has been done.

At CRS, I discovered on a new level that this work is a privilege: in caring for those whom God has entrusted to us we step into the daily manifestation of the biggest miracle of them all, resurrection.

"... In the Land of the Living"

I sign all of my correspondence as president of CRS with the closing, "May blessings overflow." I do that because in our work it is easy to be overtaken with the notion of scarcity. Every day and everywhere in the approximately one hundred countries in which we serve, we encounter devastating poverty and millions without the basics that they need for survival. In everything that we read and hear about water, food, clean air, and energy, we get this sense of immense shortage. Humans are willing to go to war to battle for such resources. The very poor are least able to get a portion for themselves. How can we bring sustainable solutions to them if indeed there is not enough to go around?

What we often forget when such global suffering and personal insecurity seem overwhelming is that our gifts and service draw from a bountiful world created by God. This is captured in a mural and photo display on the walls of a dining room at CRS's Baltimore headquarters. When you enter, on the left wall you see pictures of nature — water, plants, fishes, vegetables, and so forth — and the inscription, "We shall see the bounty of the LORD...." The inscription continues on the right wall: "... in the land of the living," (cf. Psalm 27:13) accompanied by illustrations of people enjoying these gifts of nature. This installation reminds me that our work is simply to make accessible the bounty of God to every person. We do not create these gifts, but we can help make them available to people who, for various reasons, cannot get to the table overflowing with God's bounty or to the river teeming with fish He has provided.

God is not stingy. He did not create a world based on the principle of scarcity in a zero-sum economy. Christ, in His first miracle, changed water into the *finest* wine to celebrate a marriage (John 2:1–12). When He instructed Simon to recast the net into the Lake of Gennesaret, the weight of the catch nearly broke the net (Luke 5:1–6). The leftovers alone from the multiplication of the five loaves and two fishes filled twelve baskets, a number in Jewish tradition that represents completeness (Matthew 14: 13–21).

In the gross deprivation and suffering we encounter in our work at CRS, it is not God's bounty that is absent or in short supply; it is errors of the human community that keep that bounty off of too many tables. These errors are the result, through commission or omission, of a lack of knowledge, rejection of the common good, careless stewardship, or willful and brutal destruction. "God gave the earth to the whole human race for the sustenance of all its members, without excluding or favoring anyone" (31), Pope St. John Paul II wrote in the 1991 encyclical *Centesimus Annus*, issued on the one hundredth anniversary of Pope Leo XIII's *Rerum Novarum*.

A study showed that worldwide we waste or lose perhaps a third of all food. I hardly have to tell you that in America food is thrown away from our tables in our homes every day. The food that God's bounty provides in parts of Africa where we work can spoil because there is no efficient way to get products to the market. We must be better stewards of that bounty. If we collectively erode our environment and continue to ignore the evidence of climate change, we stand to lose major coastal cities to rising sea levels, agricultural outputs to increasingly intense and frequent natural disasters, and rivers and other natural elements to rising temperatures.

Economic growth must include benefits for the poorest segments of society. It must develop human and social capital as well as responsible and transparent governance, or it will not achieve the flourishing of its full potential — of people and physical assets — equal to what God has provided. Instead it will spawn violent conflicts around the world as environmental tensions rise and the number of man-made weapons increases.

We must never forget, dismiss, or underappreciate the richness of God's world. Our work is not to make up for what God has failed to provide, but to remove the obstacles that prevent these natural endowments, our joint heritage, from working for people. Our work at CRS would be unsustainable if it was simply to help our beneficiaries fight for a share of an underresourced and diminishing world. No, our work is to help people access this bounty that God has provided, that he continues to provide every day.

The Bounty of Technology

Today, one of the ways we multiply the loaves and fishes is through technology. Whether we are using rugged laptop computers to track the battle against a disease threatening the cassava crop — a much-used staple in East Africa — or cell phones to connect pregnant women with health information in India, the use of technology expands our ability to reach those in need while focusing our efforts in ways that make them more effective.

This effort is called ICT4D — Information and Communication Technology for Development. For CRS, our emphasis on these methods is part of our commitment to the poor, to affirming that the poor deserve our best. CRS first sponsored a conference about ICT4D in Washington, D.C., in 2010. Only a handful of people showed up for the day-long event. But interest in this technological approach exploded. In 2014, more than four hundred people — staff from humanitarian organizations, donors who support this work, educators, government representatives, and technology providers — spent three days in Nairobi at a CRS-sponsored conference discussing the ways in which ICT4D-driven innovations are building resilience in developing communities.

Here's an example. In Gambia, West Africa, CRS was using ICT4D computers to register and track those receiving mosquito nets in an ambitious antimalaria campaign that aimed to distribute one net for every two people in the country. The computers helped us discover that the census numbers we were using were inaccurate. Whole villages had not been counted. So, though it was not the point of the project, we were able to provide accurate population data to government authorities. That should improve the coverage of this project and help in future efforts of all sorts — health, education, social services — whether by the government or other humanitarian groups.

Portable technologies allow greater efficiency and accuracy registering people for various programs, whether it be food distribution or space at a refugee camp. When cell phones first came to the United States, they were seen as luxuries, an addition to the ubiquitous home phone. Not so in Africa, where many communities were never wired for the telephones we grew up with. It was cell phone technology that provided an affordable form of instant communication for millions of Africans who had never had such access. That's why you see these phones in the hands of so many poor people. Your instinct might be to think that such a phone is a luxury, but it is not in that context. It is a necessity for communication that can also fight poverty. These phones provide groups like CRS with an invaluable tool, as they can be used for everything from teaching reading to informing expectant mothers about proper prenatal care to keeping farmers up to date on the prices they should be getting for their crops.

The possibilities are manifold. While we certainly face enormous challenges, our natural world and our human intelligence manifest the endowments of God that allow access to His bounty for everyone. The limiting factor is not God's generosity, but our individual willingness to step up to examine our habits, to share more generously of what we have, to dedicate our intelligence to the common good, and to use our voice for those who are excluded.

May blessings overflow.

CHAPTER TWELVE

Entertaining Angels

As I learned more about the work of CRS, so much more than I ever knew before, I realized how much of it follows a straight line from those initial efforts for the Polish people who found themselves on the Iranian border in 1943. Every year, every day, since those displaced by World War II (including my parents) were resettled, thousands more have found themselves forced to leave their homes.

The reasons vary. Sometimes it is because of conflict and violence — sometimes, drought — sometimes, storms or earthquakes or flooding. But whatever the cause, CRS has always been there to help, welcoming the stranger as the Bible tells us to.

The Old Testament book of Leviticus states clearly: "You shall treat the alien who resides with you no differently than the natives born among you; you shall love the alien as yourself; for you too were once aliens in the land of Egypt" (19:34).

And in the Gospel of Matthew we read: "For I was hungry and you gave me food, I was thirsty and you gave me drink, a stranger and you welcomed me, naked and you clothed me" (25:35–36).

The fate of those forced from their homes — in 1943 or today — is a reminder of the point Jesus makes in the Gospel of Matthew: "Whatever you did for one of these least brothers of mine, you did for me" (25:40).

"Do not neglect hospitality," the Letter to the Hebrews says, "for through it some have unknowingly entertained angels" (13:2).

Yes, where we see squalor and poverty and need of such magnitude that it might make us want to turn our heads away and look elsewhere, the Bible reminds us that there may well be angels.

One aside about etymology. Most people define a refugee as someone who is forced from his home and seeking refuge elsewhere. But in the international relief and development world, such people are divided into two types — internally displaced people (those who are still in their native country) and refugees (those who have crossed the border into another country).

Sometimes working at CRS can make you feel that you are drowning in acronyms. I might go to a meeting about an emergency response and hear that we are working with OCHA to hand out NFIs to IDPs. Oftentimes I would need simultaneous translation to know what was going on. OCHA is the United Nations' Office of Coordination of Humanitarian Affairs, which works on the ground in emergencies to see that all the needs are met. NFI means non-food items, usually household supplies, cooking pots and utensils, water containers, and soap and other sanitation materials that people leave behind when fleeing their homes. IDPs are internally displaced people, thus not refugees; otherwise we would be dealing with UNHCR (the United Nations High Commissioner for Refugees).

This distinction between IDPs and refugees has important legal ramifications. Refugees have a particular status under international treaties, giving them certain rights and restrictions. IDPs are still under the laws and regulations of their homeland.

We work with many people who have been forced from their homes, both refugees and the internally displaced. Sometimes that work is in hastily constructed camps that spring up spontaneously, as in Haiti following the 2011 earthquake when tens of thousands fled their damaged and destroyed homes. Others are situations years in the making, such as in Darfur in western Sudan where violence drove tens of thousands from their homes into camps big and small. And sometimes it's somewhere in between, such as in Dadaab, the camp in Kenya that suddenly found itself swamped with newcomers fleeing neighboring Somalia when a drought and continued political instability brought famine to the surrounding region.

The reality is often the same whether you are a refugee or an IDP. If you have to leave your home, you have entered into a situation that is fraught with uncertainty. You have left behind the familiar and safe, replacing them with the unfamiliar, with dangers that might lurk around every corner.

I feel for these people in a personal way. Growing up in Hong Kong, I was surrounded by many people who, like my parents, were essentially refugees having fled their homes in China. In my early years, our home was often a way station for those leaving China, fleeing the Cultural Revolution in the 1960s. And looming in the future for all of us was the 1996 handover of Hong Kong to the Chinese. There was an air of uncertainty about our citizenship status, indeed about our lives. Because of this, I can understand something of the refugees' plight.

And when I came to America, while of course I was no refugee, I did experience what it is like to be so far from home, amid strangers, a different culture, different values, and different ways of communicating and relating. If I felt threatened and lonely under those circumstances, imagine how those forced from their homes feel.

One thing I did not know until I came to CRS was that the agency actually served in Hong Kong during the years of my childhood. In fact, in 1955, Fr. Paul Duchesne, who was the head of CRS programming in Hong Kong, called the city the largest displaced persons camp in the world because it was filled with so many who had fled the Communist regime in China.

There was another man who worked for CRS, Fr. John Romaniello, a Maryknoll priest during the years I was being educated by the Maryknoll Sisters. Part of his job was distributing flour, cornmeal, and powdered milk provided by the United States government through the Food for Peace program. In America, many might make bread out of these ingredients. But the Chinese refugees did not eat bread, and many were paying shopkeepers to turn their food allotment into noodles.

Fr. Romaniello rounded up a dozen electric noodle machines. The product became so popular among the refugees that he became known as "The Noodle Priest." He saw it as a payback. "For centuries, my Italian forbears enjoyed spaghetti, the food brought back from China by Marco Polo," he said. "I brought noodles to the Chinese at the rate of millions of pounds a year."

There are so many places in the world where CRS, acting on the Church's biblical tradition of welcoming strangers, helps the displaced and refugees. In Darfur, the Sudanese government forced many international humanitarian organizations to leave. CRS was able to continue working. Under difficult conditions and tough deadlines, we stepped up our efforts to make sure tens of thousands were getting food and other essentials.

When the Somalis began arriving by the tens of thousands in Dadaab, we worked to construct proper sanitation facilities at a new refugee camp and educated the people about proper sanitation. Without the facilities and appropriate education, disease could easily spread due to the crowded conditions — diarrhea is one of the leading causes of death among children in the type of unsanitary circumstances that can develop in a camp.

What we try to keep in mind at CRS is that these refugees do not arrive to completely blank spaces on the map. They always have an impact on the communities that host them. Usually, these communities do more than that — they welcome them. This was certainly the case in Liberia a few years ago when refugees came across the border from Ivory Coast fleeing political violence. There, many were returning the favor as Ivorians had hosted members of their families when such violence upended peace in Liberia years before.

Most of the tens of thousands fleeing the civil war in Syria did not end up in formal camps but were absorbed into cities in Lebanon and Jordan. Around Dadaab, many of the Kenyan communities faced the same challenges brought on by drought that had driven Somalis to leave their homeland.

In such cases, CRS also provides help to the host communities to relieve their burdens, whether it is water for the drought, food to feed the extra mouths, or cash grants needed to pay rents jacked up by an influx of people.

In our work with the displaced, CRS adheres to the important principle of Integral Human Development. We understand that it is not enough to provide shelter and food, that a human being needs more substantial nourishment.

One of the biggest responses CRS ever launched to help the displaced came after the tsunami devastated countries throughout Asia on the day after Christmas in 2004. Tens of thousands of houses were destroyed. Hundreds of thousands of people were living in whatever kind of shelter they could throw together. Their worldly possessions were lost to the rage of the water. All of this occurred not just during the Christian holy season, but also during the observance of the Muslim holiday of Eid al-Adha.

When we were putting together 2,500 NFI kits (hygiene and household items) for those who lost their homes to the tsunami in the province of Aceh in northern Sumatra, Indonesia, we decided to include some additional items — a prayer mat, a sarong that is traditionally worn by men to attend the mosque, and a covering for women. All are necessary for proper observance of Eid. These "religious kits" were both a gesture of respect to the Muslims we were serving and a measure for healing, recognizing that serving those in distress means more than a tarpaulin and jerry can, more than meeting basic material needs. This was Integral Human Development in action.

When the refugees from the more recent civil war in Syria included thousands of children who had witnessed violence that their innocent eyes should never have seen — that no one's eyes should ever see — CRS knew it was not enough to provide food and shelter, or even, as we often do for displaced children, to provide education and safe places to play. So we worked with a team whose experience included years with Jim Henson of the Muppets and Sesame Street fame and came up with a video aimed at children, designed to attract their attention and engage their imagination, that would help them deal with the trauma we knew they were feeling.

Saving Lives, Reducing Risk

One advantage that we have in helping the displaced is that wherever they are, CRS — and the Church — are probably already there. Because CRS is present and active in so many countries, the likelihood is that when refugees arrive, we already have people on the ground, established relationships with local partners, and knowledge of the terrain, the culture, the challenges, and the needs specific to that locale.

In Haiti, after the earthquake devastated Port-au-Prince in 2010, hundreds of thousands were dead, and as many were without homes. Their needs were endless. CRS was running a large feeding program in the country, and we were able to divert food arriving for that program to help feed people in the many camps springing up around Port-au-Prince. One of our main facilities was in the southern part of the country and essentially undamaged by the quake. Our staff was able to head to Port-au-Prince with supplies, joining CRS colleagues already in the capital city where our headquarters building was damaged but did not collapse.

Within days, not only was CRS getting food to thousands of people who had lost their homes, but, working with local and international partners, we were able to help get a major Catholic hospital, St. Francois de Sales, where we had a program treating HIV and AIDS, up and running, caring for the injured in temporary tents set up in the courtyard amid the collapsed hospital buildings.

One of the biggest disasters to hit in the years of my presidency was Typhoon Haiyan, which pounded the Philippines in November 2013. It was as if a tornado hundreds of miles wide had roared across several of the islands of this nation, leaving behind a wide swath of destruction. Some said Haiyan had the fastest recorded winds ever to make landfall.

CRS had established deep roots in the Philippines — it is our longest-running continuous program, dating back to the days of post–World War II relief — and we were again able to respond quickly, overcoming all sorts of logistical obstacles to get help to the affected areas.

If you were paying attention to television at the time, you probably saw many pictures of the city of Tacloban that took a direct hit from the storm, both from its winds and rain and the waters the storm forced into the city from the sea. Tacloban was flattened like a pancake. As the biggest city directly in Haiyan's path, it also became the center for media activity. What we found was that with Tacloban's airport and all the media attention, many aid and relief agencies were already at work or planning to go to work there. So we headed for other areas where there might not have been as many cameras and reporters but there was still plenty of destruction and need. Within days, thousands of Filipinos in equally damaged cities south of Tacloban were sleeping under tarpaulins, often stretched over the walls of their roofless homes, provided by CRS. We worked to supply them with food, water, and needed items they had lost to the storm. Our staff was working out of the Catholic Church compound in Palo, which was sheltering many of the displaced in its damaged buildings.

One feature of CRS's response to devastation such as Haiyan or the Haitian earthquake is that we are generally there before the TV cameras arrive, and we stay long after they leave. For instance, in the Philippines, you might remember Haiyan, but do you remember Bopha? That was another powerful typhoon that struck less than a year before Haiyan, mainly affecting the island of Mindanao, where

CRS already had many programs. Over one thousand died and tens of thousands were homeless. Acres and acres of crops were destroyed in floods and landslides.

We were still at work with those affected by Bopha when Haiyan hit. Many on Mindanao were living in temporary homes we had helped construct. We were pleased when those structures proved strong enough to survive when the winds of Haiyan reached Mindanao.

And this brings up another important aspect of our approach to disasters — we plan ahead to reduce risk. We can't steer the storm away from land or calm the tsunami wave, but we can build structures that can survive hurricanes and typhoons in places where they are likely to land. We can — and do — teach people what to do, where to go to outlive the danger. We help put in place building codes for structures that can withstand earthquakes.

CRS has a team called Disaster Risk Reduction that works on these issues. When they do their job right, you don't hear about them because they have averted a catastrophe. There are no headlines and no cameras or reporters because there is no news. Often, this is as simple as working with a community on a disaster plan so that they know who goes where when trouble hits. Sometimes it is showing people how to build a house that will stay above floodwaters and be easily cleaned out when mud coats the floor. Sometimes it is helping people understand where they should store food and essential items so that they can be easily retrieved after a disaster. Other times it is training a rescue squad so that the community knows how to make tourniquets and stretchers from available materials.

Disaster risk reduction can also be work on a larger scale. Consider that after Hurricane Andrew struck southern Florida in 1992, causing widespread destruction, the state of Florida adopted more stringent building codes in storm-prone areas. The result was less destruction from subsequent hurricanes. Also remember that only a few months after the earthquake devastated Haiti, one of similar strength struck in Chile. Though it was powerful and caused a great deal of damage, there was nothing like the devastation seen in Haiti. Why? They had better building codes in place, so their structures had been designed to withstand such shocks. The temporary shelters we built on Mindanao after Typhoon Bopha weren't of the highest quality, but they were strong enough to help avoid disaster when Typhoon Haiyan hit.

You may recall the horrific images that came out of Ethiopia in the mid-1980s as drought led to famine in that land. In response, CRS took the lead to organize humanitarian organizations, working with the government of Ethiopia and international donors, to see that this would not happen again. A steady supply of food, mainly from the United States government, was secured. CRS was in charge of distributing it as needed around the nation. New agricultural practices were introduced to the region to ensure that there would not be another famine of this magnitude.

At the same time, the United States government was instrumental in creating FEWSNET — the famine early warning system — that analyzes various data, particularly rainfall, and then predicts when regions are going to have trouble producing enough food. The result: intervention can occur before famine sets in.

In 2011, when drought hit East Africa, the only place to reach famine status was Somalia, where activities by militants kept humanitarian aid out. This was the situation that forced tens of thousands to flee to Dadaab. CRS was able to use long-standing relationships to get aid inside of Somalia, though the lack of security meant that we did not publicize this work.

My point is that at CRS we understand that the best way to deal with disasters is to take action before they happen. And we are at work every day trying to do just that. It is work that does not make headlines, and it does not bring in huge donations, but it is certainly God's work.

All this comes out of the seed that was planted seventy years ago when CRS was founded — we knew then and we know now that the Gospel tells us we must help those devastated by disasters and emergencies, both natural and man-made.

As we began our strategic review for CRS, we planned to identify what we termed Strategic Program Areas. These were the areas of humanitarian work where CRS could bring extensive expertise to high-quality, sustainable, and scalable solutions to transform the lives of our beneficiaries, the capabilities of our Church partners, and knowledge of the development sector. It soon became clear that one of these areas had to be responding to emergencies. For in that work, we knew that we may well be entertaining angels.

CHAPTER THIRTEEN

"When I Was Hungry ..."

There is nothing more basic than bread — our daily bread, necessary for life, celebrated in the transubstantiation of the Eucharist as the body of Christ.

As we have noted, some 800 million people face hunger every day now, and food demand is expected to double in the next thirty years. Arable land, however, will grow only by 10 percent — and that formula does not take into account the effects of erosion and climate change. But we also know that we have the ability to feed everyone from God's bounty.

Some 500 million smallholder farm families around the world live at subsistence level — eating what they grow, nothing more. They go hungry almost every year, when their stores of food start to run out as they wait for a new harvest. Children in these families bear the marks of insufficient nutrition, affecting their mortality as well as every aspect of their ability to reach full potential — physical, mental, psychological. Their subsistence existence often means there is no money to pay school fees. Without education, they too will probably be consigned to a life of bare subsistence. The cycle will continue for another generation.

To help address this reality, in our agricultural sector we work with local communities and various institutions — governments, multilateral agencies, research centers, universities, and other nonprofits — to improve planting and growing practices; introduce seed varieties or new crops appropriate to the specific conditions; broaden the diversity of crops to extend growing seasons, restore nutrients, and reduce vulnerability that comes with growing only a single crop; enable access to water and the use of appropriate irrigation methods; enhance productivity while conserving the land and reversing erosion; and to empower farmers through education, market information, formation of co-ops, and advocacy to the government for infrastructure development and legal rights.

It was clear early on that agriculture would be one of most important strategic areas for CRS as we claim the future. Our work there is so fundamental to those we serve and so important to many areas of the agency that it must remain in the forefront.

Let me tell you about a farmer in Nicaragua, Ernesto. He dreaded hearing the sound of a motorcycle because that always meant a loan officer — the only people he knew who could afford such transportation — was coming to his farm to collect on a loan that Ernesto knew he could not repay. Like all the farmers around him, like those who came before him, Ernesto grew corn on an ancestral plot of less than five acres. At the beginning of every growing season, he borrowed money for seeds and whatever else he would need for his crop, including, he thought, chemical fertilizer. Repaying the money was the problem. Everyone in his area was growing corn so there was an oversupply there. And Ernesto didn't have the ability to transport his crop to markets where there was demand. Besides, the quality of his corn was inconsistent, which made finding buyers even more of a problem.

Still, Ernesto kept borrowing every year because he knew no other way. This put him deep in debt, the interest charges compounding his plight. He faced the loss of his farm. His family would become homeless. His teenage children would have to drop out of school. He would have no choice other than to wander from farm to farm offering his services as a day laborer. That would crush his dignity and probably not provide enough income for his family to live on.

Then Ernesto signed up for a program that CRS, working with local partners, was implementing with funds from the United States Agency for International Development. He learned about another crop, passion fruit. It could be sold on the export market. In the program, Ernesto received intensive training in cultivating passion fruit, as well as free seeds and ongoing consultation. After the first year of growing this new crop, Ernesto had earned enough in passion fruit profits to retire his debts and pay for the seeds and other supplies he needed for the second year. Along the way, he learned about methods for rotating crops to allow different sections of his farm to regain fertility.

Seeing that seedlings that are grown to three inches tall and transplanted into the field produce significantly higher yields than planting directly from seeds, Ernesto built a greenhouse to provide such seedlings for himself and other farmers. He continued to attend training classes and earned certification in using and testing agricultural chemicals. What he learned allowed him to turn away the salespeople whose pricey chemical products had impoverished both him and his land. Ernesto's success meant his two children could stay in school, even attend college. He started training and mentoring other farmers. And now the sound of a motorcycle in his neighborhood might come from one of the two he owns.

Ernesto's story does not stop there. His greenhouses needed rich and healthy soil. A group of women in the

community organized a business to provide that by collecting cow manure to feed earthworms that in turn loosen,
aerate, and fertilize soil, getting it ready for the greenhouses.

I saw the products of this soil — of God's bounty
unleashed by the hands and minds of men and women,
multiplied by the Holy Spirit — a luscious lineup of green,
healthy, robust plantings that would eventually provide the
livelihoods of many farmers and feed even more of us across
the ocean as we enjoy our passion fruit juice.

At CRS, we see this bounty in many ways, from new
varieties of rice developed by scientists that can adapt to
drought, floods, and salinity — all major calamities that
tend to hit rice-growing areas — leading to dramatic increases in yield, to simple ventilated pits that allow Afghan
farmers to preserve many more of the potatoes they store
underground during the winter. In the Philippines, low-
cost rain shelters made of plastic sheeting stretched over
wooden stilts enable onions that once would have been lost
to storm damage to instead ripen for sale in markets. The
rainwater accumulating in the plastic sheets is collected into
and flows through small channels where tilapia are grown,
providing additional income as well as fertilizer. In Sub-Saharan Africa, CRS is pursuing a large-scale opportunity in
climate-smart agriculture that entails planting trees next to
crops, thus providing shade, preventing erosion, and adding nutrients to the soil.

One thing I quickly learned at CRS was that moving
into the humanitarian world did not mean leaving the business world behind. While many might see what we do as
charity in the traditional form of handing out food, water,
shelter, and other essentials, that is only a small part of our
mission. We understand that market forces are powerful,
much more powerful than anything we can bring to bear.

Much of our work, therefore, involves trying to make those market forces work in service to the poor and vulnerable.

Where I grew up in Hong Kong, we had almost no arable land. There was no way the population could feed itself. If we were going to survive, we had to rely on business. Hong Kong is where I saw the great things business could do, how it could empower people and free them from shackles that otherwise would have limited their lives, how it could create economies that would lift up even the lowliest.

But I also saw the other side of business, those whom the system had discarded, leaving them at the mercy of forces they could not control. These could be accidents that severed their fingers, or tuberculosis, which prevented them from working, or owners who pay them the legal but insufficient minimum wage. I realized that business is not intrinsically good or evil. It depends on the people who lead it. I came to understand that business is too great a power and has too much potential for lifting up people to be allowed to exist without a firm base in ethics. That is what I dedicated myself to during my decades in business education, instilling ethics in the business leaders of the future. And now at CRS, I got to see another aspect of business, of the market, as we tried to harness those powers for the good of the poor.

As Pope Francis said in his 2013 apostolic exhortation *Gaudium Evangelii,* "Business is a vocation, and a noble vocation, provided that those engaged in it see themselves challenged by a greater meaning in life; this will enable them truly to serve the common good by striving to increase the goods of this world and to make them more accessible to all" (203).

Do not ever forget that integrity and success are not trade-offs. Success without integrity will not last long, and it is a form of poverty: moral poverty. When Jesus said,

"Blessed are the meek, for they will inherit the land (Matthew 5:5)," he may well have had successful people in mind. Too often we think meek means weak. But it actually means humble. Those are strong leaders: they have respect for people, appreciate colleagues' gifts and contributions, and acknowledge their own gaps and dependence on others. Arrogance is not strength. Arrogance in business can lead to the kind of fiscal disaster we saw in the Global Financial Crisis of 2007. Meekness leads to long-term success. So blessed are the meek, indeed.

Building Resilience

Working with subsistence farmers, one of our main goals is to build resilience. Too often these people live on the edge, hungry when awaiting every harvest and then only one bad rainfall away from malnutrition, from needing handouts to see their families survive and thrive. How can that hand-to-mouth cycle be broken? With resilience that comes with a culture and habit of saving.

Sometimes that means saving crops so that a bad harvest does not mean disaster. We work with farmers on better storage techniques.

It can also mean saving money that will allow a farmer to buy food for his family in times of lean or missing harvests. One of the best ways for a farmer to do that is the way Ernesto did it, growing enough crops — and the right crops — so that he can sell them in the market and build up a safety net. CRS works to make this happen around the world. It can be on a small scale that might involve a surplus sold in a village market; or on a large scale, such as in the Philippines where CRS has helped small farmers join together so that they can sell their onion crop to Jollibee, the largest fast-food chain in the country; or in Ethiopia, where CRS has linked bean farmers to the international export market; or in Central America where CRS works with coffee farmers to meet the international market standards demands, as well as to ensure that they get a fair price, and a fair profit, from their crop.

But there are other ways as well. In poor villages in Afghanistan, CRS sponsored women's self-help groups. There was no shortage of women who were interested in earning money. CRS helped start small home-based businesses by providing training and supplies like sewing machines, baking ovens, sugar and flour, thread and fabric, working capital, and a simple tracking system. Khaire lived in the remote village of Chaghcharan. Her women's group began by raising chickens and selling their eggs. Then the twenty women saw an opportunity in the marketplace — their town had no bakery.

So, with the help of CRS, they got two ovens and what was supposed to be enough supplies for three months. Khaire reported that the bakery had so many orders, the supplies were used up in ten days. Their biggest customers are the Afghan policemen who, like fellow law enforcement officers around the world, enjoy a good doughnut-equivalent. Two months later, the bakery was self-sufficient, each of the twenty women taking home $8 a week in profits. Khaire said that the money means her children have enough to eat. "Now I can buy more food," she said. "My children have gained weight."

One very simple innovation pioneered by CRS is called the keyhole garden. Essentially, it's a small raised garden shaped like a keyhole, built out of local stone with a central point for adding water and fertilizer. It originated in southern Africa as part of our HIV and AIDS response. The design allows a person to stand rather than bend or kneel while gardening. Hence, people who were too sick to go to the fields could still grow crops, even if they used a wheelchair. But it proved so effective that these gardens are now spreading around the world. For one thing, their crops tend to be green vegetables, which add needed nutrients to diets that are often dominated by a starchy staple — rice, corn, or cassava. For another thing, the crops grown in a keyhole garden are often unusual for the area, so they have a value in the market.

A keyhole garden becomes a way for even the sick and infirm to improve their diet and make money, adding to their resilience. This is a lifeline for the person's health because patients on HIV-AIDS medication need twice the nutritional intake if the drugs are to be effective.

Letima lives in a remote area of Lesotho, the tiny landlocked country in the midst of South Africa. The seventh of eight children, Letima was used to poverty, but he did have enough to eat.

"After the death of my father, life changed," he said. His father died of AIDS — Lesotho has a high rate of HIV infection. "Food was the problem."

A CRS-funded program provided Letima and his family with food support and showed them how to build and maintain a keyhole garden, which increased the variety and nutrition of the food he and his siblings ate.

"We were able to have three meals a day," he said.

In keeping with Integral Human Development concepts, the program did more, providing books and shoes so that the now better-nourished Letima and his siblings could return to school.

"We were like all the other schoolchildren who were not orphans," he said. "My life became better."

The Power of Capital

One of my favorite CRS programs is called Savings and Internal Lending Community, or SILC. Like keyhole gardens, part of its strength is its simplicity. But every day, SILC programs are transforming lives around the world.

SILC is essentially a savings club formed by people who are too poor to participate in the formal financial sector. The basic concept has been practiced in many folk cultures across centuries, but CRS scaled up the formation of these groups and provided the training necessary for them to succeed. You have probably heard of microlending and what a boon that has been to the poor around the world. But millions are too poor to qualify even for those loans. They have no assets, no collateral, no contact with the formal financial sector at all. This is where SILC steps in.

A SILC group comprises a dozen or so members of a community. As a group, they decide on all their rules. At the outset that means who joins and how much money each member will contribute every week, as well as who will take on the specific tasks needed to keep the group going. A certain percentage of the funds are set aside to help members or the community in the case of an emergency. Most of the money goes into their "bank" — a box with three locks to hold it shut. One member takes the box home after every meeting. Three others have the keys. To open the box, all four must be present and participating.

After the money is collected, it is available for loans to the members. Again, the SILC is self-governing. As a group, the members decide if a loan is approved; they decide on interest rates; they decide on payback schedules. At the end of a cycle, usually a year, the group divides up the profits among themselves.

When you work with the extremely poor, you begin to understand in a fundamental way something that those in big business know very well — that the ability to accumulate capital is crucial to economic success. But there is precious little chance for the very poor to do that. All money that comes in goes out immediately, almost always for the purchase of necessities. If you have enough for your family, there is always someone in your extended family — aunts, uncles, cousins — who needs help.

Imagine the hottest, driest desert. If you took a bucket of water and poured it into that terrain, it would disappear, never to be seen again. That is what happens to capital among the poorest of the poor. The model among wealthier people is to pour water into a stream behind a dam where it can build up like a lake. Once that happens, you have a usable amount of capital, and it can make a difference in so many ways — whether it means funding for a new business or the ability to bounce back from an unexpected shock to your economic system.

Through SILC, members — and I am proud to say that the overwhelming majority of them are women — usually have access to capital for the first time in their lives. And what they do with it is what people in capitalist economies so often do; they use it to create more capital.

I heard of many women in SILC groups who took their borrowed money and bought chickens. With those they started an egg business. Profits were first used to pay back the loan and then went to business expansion — more chickens, more eggs, perhaps some employees. I heard of many other small businesses started the same way.

There was a woman in Ethiopia who used SILC funding to buy a steer. She fattened it up and sold it at a profit. Then she bought another one and did the same thing. She was on the third when I met her. With some of her profits, she has established a small hairdressing business for her eldest daughter in the front of her housing compound.

I often heard of skepticism that accompanied the beginning of a SILC group. Having never saved any money, the members would agree to put in only the smallest amount each week, really just a few cents. But after they went through their first cycle of lending and borrowing — and then splitting up the profits — the next time around they would each put in a few more dollars. They had come to understand the power of capital in a way I could only hope my business students would.

With such success, it is not surprising to report that more than one million people have joined up for CRS SILC groups and saved $10 million. And they continue to sign up — more every year.

SILC is hardly the only way we see the use of business principles in our work. In the wake of the earthquake in Haiti, CRS fed tens of thousands of people who lived in the crowded camps. But we also monitored the local markets. Once food began to appear in substantial quantities, we cut back on our food distributions, eventually eliminating them. Some criticized that, saying we weren't helping those in need. But one thing we never want to do is undercut the local market. We know that the local markets are a much more efficient way of distributing food, of getting it to the people. And we also want to spur local food production. If farmers can't sell their crop because the competition is free food, they won't produce it.

What we then turned to instead of food distribution was cash-for-work programs, paying people to clear rubble, to empty drainage ditches, to do the many tasks that restored the devastated city. That money could then be used to purchase goods in the markets, stimulating the economy, helping everyone.

We did many other things to help the economy in Haiti after the earthquake. For instance, Léopold lost his house in Port-au-Prince, and with it his home-based bakery. He spent months living without shelter or basic essentials. CRS worked with Léopold and people in his neighborhood, building a transitional shelter where he could live and get his bakery up and running. With a $500 small business grant from CRS, Léopold bought an industrial-sized sifter and enough one-hundred-pound bags of flour to get his bakery going again. He went back into business, hiring five people from his community.

We recognized that the key to helping Haitians after the earthquake was not handouts in the temporary camps, but job creation, so we provided loans, grants, and business training to hundreds of entrepreneurs like Léopold; like Inola, who began to support her family through sales of the peanut butter she makes; and like Ulysee, whose leather-crafts business expanded enough for him to take on an apprentice.

In a win-win-win program, CRS loaned a hand-operated rubble crusher to another entrepreneur under an agreement that CRS would purchase the crushed rubble at a fixed price to use in cement for the foundations of houses to be built. That woman rapidly expanded her business, so much so that she eventually had a dozen employees collecting the rubble from the destroyed buildings, running the crusher, and bagging the sand. Rubble was cleared, the economy was stimulated, and Haitians were taking care of themselves. This program engaged quite a number of first-time entrepreneurs.

Sometimes the payoff for using these business principles goes far beyond dollars and cents. For instance, for

SILC groups, CRS provides the training to start the group and then gives support and advice for the first cycle, usually about a year. Then we leave it up to the group. Nearly all of them continue. And the SILC model is self-sustaining in part because as we move to a second stage of scaling up, we use a different model — training and certifying Private Service Providers, local people who help SILC groups get started and then advise them while they get off the ground. They get a fee from each group for this work and can take on apprentices. SILC is so popular that the Private Service Providers say they don't have to market their services; people come to them because they want to start a SILC group.

This model is important because the growth of SILC groups no longer depends on the grants and donations CRS receives. For CRS to serve as many people as possible, we have to remove ourselves from the picture so that we don't become the bottleneck in a project's progress. This is the classic "working ourselves out of a job if we are successful." Assessment indicates that this model of the Private Service Provider is well-received and taking off. As SILC groups achieve success, some of them also gain access to formal institutions like microlending banks. We started the Private Service Provider model in Kenya but hope to spread it around the world.

This is important to us in all the work we do: we want to leave behind something that will last, that will continue to help the community, often in ways that we never intended or envisioned. When a committee is formed to run a water project — to set the rates, to ensure maintenance, to hire staff — this might be the first time that a community has seen the power of acting together in an organized way. This can lead to other projects like building a wall, a dam, a cannery, or advocating for the village with local and national government, the first steps to a real civil society.

Another way SILC resonates was evident in that Ethiopian group, the one with the woman who bought and sold steers and set her daughter up with a hairdressing business. Its members were all people affected by HIV and AIDS. Some were HIV positive. Others had lost parents to AIDS. The woman who bought the steers had lost her husband; she was using her loans and profits to set her children up in business so that they could survive without their father.

The SILC group served as more than a savings club for these people. It was a place they could talk about HIV and AIDS, where they could be comfortable and free of stigmatization. They could be honest. They could be supportive. They also branched out in their learning to cover topics related to health, nutrition, and child-rearing. Along the way many gained basic literacy and arithmetic skills. It was a therapy group and a safe haven, as well as an important part of their economic well-being. It is ironic in that when we visited one such side group of individuals with HIV and AIDS, we found that their success had made them the envy of their village.

SILC groups often serve such purposes. One of the most moving I ever saw was in Rwanda, where a SILC group brought together perpetrators of the 1994 genocide with family members of its victims. The business of this SILC group was mediation, and they were able to form relationships and to bridge gaps that many would think unbridgeable. But I saw them bridged. I saw them embrace. I saw them take responsibility. I saw them reconcile.

Once again, I saw a miracle.

CHAPTER FOURTEEN

The Lazarus Effect

CRS first responded to the pandemic of HIV and AIDS in 1989 in Uganda, joining a worldwide response by the Church to this horrific disease that was killing so many. At the time there was little to be done beyond giving its victims the care and dignity they deserved. Some had been shunned by their communities, by their families. They deserved respect as members of God's family. They were our neighbors.

A decade later, drug regimens were being identified that could keep the deadly virus at bay, but they remained so expensive that there was no way they could have a significant impact on the population served by CRS and the Church, as well as other humanitarian organizations, in Africa and elsewhere around the world.

This began to change in 2003 with the passage of the President's Emergency Plan for AIDS Relief, or PEPFAR. This committed the resources of the United States to the fight against HIV and AIDS in poorer countries. Specifically, it made these new drugs — called antiretrovirals — available for the common person for the first time.

With a number of partners, CRS formed a coalition known as AIDSRelief that won a grant from PEPFAR to administer programs in ten countries — eight in Africa, plus Haiti and Guyana to our south. This was a transformative event, not only for the millions served by AIDSRelief, but also for CRS. Working in some of the poorest countries on

Earth, AIDSRelief put almost four hundred thousand people on antiretroviral therapy. Putting patients on the therapy is only the first step. For these drugs to be successful, they must be taken regularly, without fail. In fact, it is a real setback if someone doesn't stick to the program, because it allows the virus to develop immunities to the treatment, meaning that even stronger and more expensive drugs must be used to combat it.

Our main partner in the AIDSRelief consortium was the University of Maryland's Institute of Human Virology, headed by Robert Gallo, one of the leading experts on HIV and AIDS in the world. The Institute is only a few blocks from CRS's headquarters in Baltimore. In the span of those blocks was one of the greatest concentrations of knowledge of how to combat this virus, knowledge that covered the spectrum from the theoretical to the applied, from research on the subcellular level to effectively delivering the results of that research to people in need around the world.

PEPFAR had many critics in the United States, including those who said it would be beyond the ability of poor Africans to stick to the complicated schedule required by antiretroviral therapy. But in its eight years of existence, AIDSRelief had figures for adherence — those who kept to their schedules for taking medications — that exceeded the numbers recorded by similar programs in the United States.

We were able to accomplish this because CRS had the privilege of working with local partners, especially Church partners. That provided a pool of volunteers — often parishioners — who became our community health workers. After training, they would fan out into their neighborhoods where they made regular checks of those on HIV medication to see that they were taking it on schedule and had enough, to answer their questions, and to solve their problems.

When antiretroviral therapy first appeared, it was said to produce "the Lazarus effect" because these drugs had the ability to take people who were on the verge of death and restore them to health. Some of them entered a hospice to live out their last days but then walked out under their own power once they received ART (antiretroviral therapy), reoriented to living instead of preparing to die. Families that had been mourning began celebrating.

Christina and Danny, both from Zambia, can tell their respective stories. Danny had spent almost a decade wasting away, but he refused to believe he had HIV, even when many urged him to get tested. His wife died. He came down with tuberculosis. His coworkers gave him a present — a blanket of a style that let him know it was for his burial. Finally, he consented to be tested and found that he did have HIV. By that time his immune system was in tatters.

Christina returned home after months away at college to find that Charles, her husband, had started another relationship and planned to take a new wife. Christina soon left, but it turned out she had already been infected.

Both Christina and Danny received antiretrovirals. As they returned to health, both sought counseling in a support group run by a partner of AIDSRelief. There they met, fell in love, and got married. Their story shows that it is one thing to bring people back to life, but it is another to help them continue their lives, seek fulfillment, and find happiness as well as health.

There was much more to PEPFAR and AIDSRelief than delivering these medications. For one, there was care for those who had HIV but did not develop AIDS, to help them live with the virus. For another, there were the many, particularly children, who lost family members to the pandemic.

Our work with what became known as OVCs — orphans and vulnerable children — reached hundreds of thousands of people. Some of them carried the virus themselves, often from birth. When both parents died, some children were lovingly cared for by grandparents and relatives. But that was not always the case.

Let me introduce you to Erick, who was born in 1979 in a region in western Kenya near the Tanzania border and Lake Victoria. It has one of the highest incidences of HIV in his country, an infection rate that was estimated at 14 percent at the time. In 1998, his father succumbed to AIDS. In 2001, the first of his father's three wives died.

"In 2002, within a day of each other, my mother died and my father's second wife died," Erick explained. "All six of my uncles were already dead, along with their wives."

That left Erick as the eldest, responsible for his seven siblings and his eight cousins.

"I had to take more responsibility, being the father, mother, and big brother to my extended family," Erick said. "Life was not easy," was the way he put it.

That statement was certainly true for Doreen as well. Also born in 1979, she moved as a young child from her rural Ugandan home to the slums of the capital city Kampa, where her father went to look for work but found none.

"With no job, he began drinking with the guys," she said. "Incidents happened, and he contracted HIV in 1986. By 1987, he had fallen sick with AIDS."

Soon, Doreen's mother, too, showed signs of the disease. She could no longer work. They lost their home and were living in a shack in the bush. "We were beggars," she said.

CRS-funded programs, implemented with local partners, turned around these lives that could have descended into despair. In 1992, Doreen found a CRS partner through a church where she went looking for help. Better food and shelter followed. And, most important to Doreen, fees for school.

She was not about to turn her back on this opportunity. She studied hard. If there was no transportation to school, she walked. She passed her exams. She moved on to secondary school and excelled there.

This woman who, as a child, was living in a shack in the bush near Kampala now has a college degree in education and is an elementary school teacher. She has married. In addition to her teaching, Doreen talks to children who, like her, are victims of HIV and AIDS, trying to give them hope.

"What I have done is because of the help of the Christian Caring Community in collaboration with CRS," she said.

Erick was in a similar situation. Three meals a day was out of reach for his family. They were down to one or two, almost always just porridge.

In 2003, Erick came across a CRS local partner, Community Development Program. He enrolled his family.

"We received food support and shelter upgrades," he said. "We had had no proper housing since my father died. We got an iron-roofed house. We received health care and school uniforms."

His younger siblings began attending primary and secondary schools. One graduated from high school and headed for college. Erick himself was too old for high school, but he borrowed money through the program to enroll in a technical school, taking a butchery course. He turned that education into a catering business that can bring in as much as $150 a month.

Erick has also started a small farm that now produces more corn than what his family needs. He gives some to those in need and sells the rest.

Like Doreen, Erick wants to help those in his situation, so he formed a group called Blue Cross. "It gives psycho-social support to youth affected by the impact of the HIV scourge," he explained.

There were those who tried to divert Doreen and Erick from their paths, offering to take Doreen in if she would look after their children or to take some of Erick's siblings off his hands and make them domestic workers.

Both of them refused.

"It was our parents who died," Erick said. "Not our dreams."

Through AIDSRelief, we worked to combat the stigma associated with the disease to help those who carried the virus to live with dignity and respect. And we worked to prevent mother-to-child transmission of the virus so that the next generation could live HIV free.

Christine and Danny, the couple from Zambia, can testify to that. After getting themselves healthy and properly caring for the seven children they already had, they decided they wanted a child of their own. With support and counseling from AIDSRelief partners, they followed the regimen aimed at preventing mother-to-child transmission of the virus.

"After that, Christina gave birth to a very, very beautiful baby girl," Danny said. Agatha was free of HIV. Her parents were proud and full of joy — and healthy.

PEPFAR came up for renewal in 2008, five years after it began. Our advocacy team in Washington, speaking from the knowledge gained during our years working on the ground around the world, urged not only renewal, but funding levels that would allow PEPFAR to reach beyond its original boundaries, treating diseases such as tuberculosis and malaria, which often preyed on those whose immune systems were compromised by HIV.

Along with many other groups active in this area — including the leadership at PEPFAR — we recognized that this virus could ultimately only be fought with robust local health systems. The bill finally passed by Congress provided the funding and framework to start building those.

By the time I took over as president of CRS, AIDSRelief was winding down. This was by design. From the beginning, the plan had been to hand the program over to a local partner in each country. This fit in perfectly with the CRS philosophy not only of always working through local partners, but also of always leaving behind structures and knowledge that would enhance and empower our local partners.

In fact, AIDSRelief had its first successful handover of a PEPFAR program in 2010, when we passed control of the work in South Africa to the South African Catholic Bishops Conference. CRS continued to work with the SACBC, but the SACBC took the lead in carrying out the PEPFAR mission. This was replicated in the other countries in which we served.

To me, our years of AIDSRelief work had made clear how central health is to our mission. It is an expression of our fundamental Catholic belief in the sanctity of life, from conception to natural death.

As I came to know CRS better, I also saw that during our years of AIDSRelief work we had built up a tremendous depth of expertise and experience in the health area. This was exceptional excellence that we could continue to deploy for the common good, putting Integral Human Development into action by not only combatting and preventing various diseases, but also ameliorating the many effects these diseases had on families and communities. Health would be another of our areas of emphasis as we moved the agency forward with our new strategy.

CHAPTER FIFTEEN

Full Circle

As I have said, I knew little about Catholic Relief Services before I joined our board in 2003. I soon learned what an outstanding institution CRS is, and how it really might be the "best kept secret" of the Catholic Church in the United States.

When I was a board member, I wondered if this was a good thing. More Catholics should know about this remarkable organization that they actually own, that is part of their Church. So, as president, I set out to do something about it.

In my first months at CRS, many invitations for speaking engagements came in, and I accepted almost every one of them. I practically kept a packed suitcase in my office, ready to go at a moment's notice, because I wanted to tell the CRS story to anyone who would listen. I wanted Catholics and anyone else interested to know that they could become part of this, that they could use CRS to join hands with their neighbors in God's family around the world.

I also called on our staff to reimagine and reemphasize our annual Lenten campaign, CRS Rice Bowl. Like many Catholics in America, this is where I first remember hearing about CRS, but at first I thought they were talking about something I knew well from Chinese culture.

Growing up in Hong Kong, "rice bowl" was used as an indication of overall well-being. If you say you have a "new rice bowl," you might have found a new job; an "iron rice bowl" might mean your future prosperity is assured; a "solid rice bowl" might indicate a steady job. When you use "rice bowl" this way in Chinese culture, you are really talking about your livelihood. I have found no real equivalent in American English. It is perhaps a combination of "steady paycheck" and "nest egg."

It is actually a nice way of thinking about this beautiful expression of Lent, which can help provide stability to many poor around the world. The cardboard collection box of CRS Rice Bowl can form the foundation for a lifetime not only of giving, sharing, and sacrificing, but also of real solidarity with the poor. So as an agency we came together to raise the participation in CRS Rice Bowl.

Solidarity is a concept basic to Catholic Social Teaching. The term is often thrown about in various political contexts, but in the realm of Catholic Social Teaching it has a specific meaning. As Pope St. John Paul II wrote in his 1987 encyclical *Sollicitudo Rei Socialis*, issued on the twentieth anniversary of Bl. Pope Paul VI's *Populorum Progressio*:

> [Solidarity] is not a feeling of vague compassion or shallow distress at the misfortunes of so many people, both near and far. On the contrary, it is a firm and persevering determination to commit oneself to the common good; that is to say to the good of all and of each individual, because we are all really responsible for all.

John Paul II further expounded on solidarity in his 1995 encyclical *Evangelium Vitae*, speaking of "a notion of freedom that exalts the isolated individual in an absolute way," because it "gives no place to solidarity, to openness to others and service of them…. It is precisely in this sense that Cain's answer to the Lord's question 'Where is Abel your brother?' can be interpreted: 'I do not know; am I my brother's keeper?' (Genesis 4:9). Yes, every man is his 'brother's keeper,' because God entrusts us to one another" (19).

This is what I felt so strongly when I came to CRS, when I contemplated the mysteries of God, neighbor, self. This kind of solidarity is not a mere intellectual acknowledgment that we all are members of the family of mankind. It is more an acceptance of everyone you see, and don't see, as connected to you and to each other in a way that is binding and mysterious. You truly feel the power of the Holy Spirit as God is manifest among us.

Solidarity is at the base of so much of what we do at CRS. For one, it tells us that it is not enough that we commit ourselves to the task of helping the poor around the world. We must also ask our public officials to pay attention to their plight and do something about it.

Consider the words of John XXIII in his 1961 encyclical *Mater et Magistra*:

> The solidarity that binds all men together as members of a common family makes it impossible for wealthy nations to look with indifference upon the hunger, misery, and poverty of other nations whose citizens are unable to enjoy even elementary human rights. The nations of the world are becoming more and more dependent on one another, and it will not be possible to preserve a lasting peace so long as glaring economic and social imbalances persist (157).

As Americans, we are citizens of one of the wealthiest nations on earth. As Catholics, it is our duty to ask our nation to help in this task of aiding the poor. Solidarity demands that of us.

Investing in the Poor

One of the most exciting projects I have recently been involved in links the wealth of the developed nations directly to those in need, not by encouraging traditional charitable handouts, but rather by getting those with money to invest it in a way that will offer solutions to entrenched social challenges while providing a return for the investors.

It's called Impact Investing. CRS, along with the Pontifical Commission on Justice and Peace and my former institution, Notre Dame's Mendoza College of Business, organized a conference about this emerging practice at the Vatican in 2014.

The idea is simple — you can make money by doing good. Impact investors seek two types of return on their money — financial and social. What they discover is that poor people are actually a good investment. They want to spend their money in productive ways but too often are not given the opportunity. So impact investors provide capital for an electrification enterprise in India or a community water project in Madagascar or a coffee cooperative in Guatemala. These are businesses that can provide financial return to investors while delivering needed services to the poor. They will have an impact on peoples' lives and livelihoods, enabling the development of industries powered by energy.

The purpose of the conference was to begin to understand how the Church should position itself as impact investing expands. The highlight was an audience with Pope Francis. We were all honored and humbled to meet the

Holy Father, feeling the warmth of his pastoral presence. As he said of the conference's topic:

> It is important that ethics once again play its due part in the world of finance and that markets serve the interests of peoples and the common good of humanity. It is increasingly intolerable that financial markets are shaping the destiny of peoples rather than serving their needs, or that the few derive immense wealth from financial speculation while the many are deeply burdened by the consequences.[7]

In his statement, Francis quoted from the preface of *Poor for the Poor: The Mission of the Church* by Cardinal Gerhard Muller, who said that a project like this

> acknowledges the ultimate connection between profit and solidarity, the virtuous circle existing between profit and gift.... Christians are called to rediscover, experience, and proclaim to all this precious and primordial unity between profit and solidarity. How much the contemporary world needs to rediscover this beautiful truth![8]

What a journey it had been that had led me there to the Vatican, to that meeting with the Holy Father. It began when my father took my siblings and me to church. Even though he didn't come in, he set us on the path where we could find meaning. I thought of Gaga, who raised me, who bestowed on me so many wonderful values, so much wisdom, jewels that I cherish to this day. She did for me what Francis urges for all Catholics, for everyone — to see what the world looks like from the standpoint of a servant without power and prestige. We need to see the people who have no options but to sell their children, the children who have lost their parents and are on their own, all of those who look in from the outside.

And, of course, I thought of the Maryknoll Sisters in Hong Kong, who educated me, whose dedication and reverence made God real to me. There is no way I would have been standing in the Vatican without the school they founded, without my teachers, without my classmates.

In the late 1990s, there were plans for a gathering to celebrate the seventieth anniversary of our school. Organizers solicited names of distinguished alumnae to single out for honor. All the entries that came in, not surprisingly, spoke of professional achievements. The Maryknoll Sisters decided to reframe this activity. They felt that the purpose of their work with us was to give "the girls" choices to define and follow their own dreams, and these were not restricted to professional pursuits. They wanted us to know that they were just as proud of the stay-at-home mothers, community volunteers, loving daughters who took care of our parents, government employees who served society, as they were of distinguished heads of companies or important government officials. What would have been an elitist exercise was transformed into an invitation to revel in the diverse life experiences that represented "the voices of our alumnae." Today, my friends from first grade and I — no matter where life has taken us in the years since — are in almost daily contact. We look out for each other and meet as equals and sisters. Their gift to me: the desire for grace in a competitive world.

I have also maintained close contact with the sisters. One of my favorite teachers, Sr. Helene O'Sullivan, served as the point person from Maryknoll Sisters for the investigation of the 1980 murders of the "Churchwomen of El Salvador": Maryknoll Sisters Ita Ford and Maura Clarke, the Ursuline missionary Dorothy Kazel, and lay missionary Jean Donovan. We met for lunch and discussed her experiences, including her role in testifying before Congress. Eventually it was established that their murders were ordered by those high in the government of El Salvador.

I have been to the Maryknoll motherhouse many times. It is where I connect with my spiritual roots and rekindle the sense that first came from those sisters in Hong Kong: that God just can't be far away. In the chapel there, I see many sisters now in their nineties, frail and bent over in deep devotion. I cannot help but note that their small and delicate frames, their bent bodies, tell the stories of how God makes us great. Their fidelity spawns a holiness reminding me that saints begin on earth and their destiny is within reach for each of us.

I had an unforgettable visit to the Motherhouse in 2008. I needed quiet time. The sisters insisted on placing me in the guest room right next to Mother Mary Joseph's suite, which included her office, bedroom, and bath. I have felt an affinity for Mother Mary Joseph, the Smith graduate who founded my beloved Maryknoll Sisters in 1912 and died in 1955. She and I overlapped on earth for one year. She was a big woman (and I am not petite), and she loved to laugh (which I do, too). I had access to her rooms and was to use her bathroom. On the way, when I passed by her portrait. I would bow to it each time.

By the second day, I had settled in and wanted to read her diaries, which were neatly typed and filed in the bookcases lining the wall. I sat on a chair at the back of the room, not wishing to impose myself. That feeling was hard to explain, since there was no one else there. I loved reading her entries: they were engrossing and hilarious, serious and in-spiring. She wrestled with issues big and small: how to cre-ate a community among the novices, how to live in joy and give expression to it, how to form one's faith in God. She dealt with life and death issues in decisions to send sisters to various parts of the world where pestilence, diseases, or violence had erupted. Most instructive for me, she did not write as one with all the answers, but as one who made deci-sions in the midst of trade-offs and uncertainties, often with the lives of young religious on the line. She turned to prayer.

By the third and final day of that stay, I went back to the office to "say goodbye" to Mother Mary Joseph. I was taking leave of a grandmother of sorts whose life and voca-tion were partly responsible for the person I have become. I felt this strong invitation and irresistible impulse to do something I had refrained from doing until then — sit at her desk. It was not so much out of curiosity or the thrill of con-necting with a historical artifact; it was more like receiving an heirloom from the elder in the family, an heirloom that contained the essence of what that family stood for.

What I felt that day was an invitation to step up to continue that journey that Mother Mary Joseph started long ago, a journey that over a century later still pulsates with purpose and urgency. Something beckoned me, the next generation, to "say yes," to not just cherish the past, but to forge a future from all the goodness, courage, and love that brought us to the present. We Maryknoll girls are the daughters in faith of the sisters. We received not only the training and education to succeed professionally and personally, but also inherited the dreams, commitment, sacrifice, and holiness that affected every aspect of our lives. What they gave us assumed a permanent home in our spirit. So, on behalf of all the Maryknoll girls, with all their diverse life experiences, I took the seat at Mother Mary Joseph's desk and made the promise to continue her journey.

What I did not know that day is that eventually that promise would lead me to sit behind another desk, in my office in Baltimore as the president of CRS. I had been reluctant to take this leap — to "say yes" as I pledged that day in the motherhouse — but now it seemed so right, so natural. Mother Mary Joseph had sent those women from America out into the world, and they had found me in Hong Kong. Because of them, because of what they taught me, I had come to America myself. And now here I was, in the birthplace of American Catholicism, guiding an organization that tries to do what she did, live the faith we so cherish in all its manifestations around the world, in solidarity with every member of God's family.

It is a joyous journey, but not always an easy one. Today, when I am making my way clumsily through the rubble to examine the reconstruction of a building destroyed in an earthquake or trekking along a rough mountainous path to see an agricultural project, always bemoaning my lack of agility, I recall photographs I saw in that library of Mother Mary Joseph poised on a donkey or a horse, making her own way through rugged and uncertain terrains, no more adept than I, but loving the adventure and looking beyond the struggles of that moment.

What a gift and a heritage she and so many have given me! We have all received similar gifts from so many who have gone before us. Let us all pray every day that we can make ourselves worthy to receive them.

AFTERWORD

By Cardinal Seán O'Malley, O.F.M. Cap.

On a Saturday evening at the end of August 2014, in the course of travelling from Boston to New York, I met Fr. Timothy Flanigan, a Catholic Deacon from the Diocese of Providence, Rhode Island, and Professor of Medicine at Brown University, who specializes in infectious diseases, and Sr. Barbara Brilliant, a Franciscan Missionary of Mary who for many years has served and ministered to the people of the Diocese of Monrovia in Liberia.

Dr. Flanigan and Sr. Barbara were taking the last scheduled flight from the United States to Liberia to go to Monrovia and assist Catholic hospitals there with the response to the Ebola crisis. As they prepared for that journey, with great faith and courage, Dr. Flanigan and Sr. Barbara asked if I could connect them with any sources of support for their mission. It took me but a moment to know that Dr. Carolyn Woo and Catholic Relief Services would be the best choice.

Within hours of our making contact, Dr. Woo and her staff were in communication with Dr. Flanigan and Sr. Barbara, providing a full report on the activities CRS had undertaken thus far to respond to the crisis, the ways they could offer assistance at the immediate moment, and establishing referrals to other sources of support.

This rapid and comprehensive response to our request for assistance was not surprising. Literally and figuratively, Dr. Woo's bags are always packed and ready to go in support of CRS and the people it serves. She is indeed dedicated to building a better world, fueled by the belief that God's providential care is present in the world, manifested in the many good works people initiate every day.

CRS and all those it serves are blessed by Dr. Woo's leadership and commitment to the mission. It is my hope that this book will provide you insight into her faith and her love of neighbor and will be an opportunity to consider support for the exemplary work of Catholic Relief Services.

NOTES

1 C. S. Lewis, "The Weight of Glory," in *The Weight of Glory and Other Addresses* (San Francisco: HarperCollins, 2001), 46.

2 www.newadvent.org/library/docs_le13rn.htm, paragraph 54.

3 www.newadvent.org/library/docs_le13rn.htm, paragraph 20.

4 Bl. Pope Paul VI, Encyclical, *Populorum Progressio* (On the Development of Peoples), March 26, 1967, www.vatican.va.

5 Bl. Pope Paul VI, Message for the Celebration of the Day of Peace, "If You Want Peace, Work for Justice," January 1, 1972, www.vatican.va.

6 Address at the Jesuit Refugee Service in Rome, September 10, 2013, www.vatican.va.

7 Address of Pope Francis, "Impact Investing for the Poor," June 14, 2014, www.vatican.va.

8 Ibid.